clutter
free

clutter free

KATHI LIPP

HARVEST HOUSE PUBLISHERS
EUGENE, OREGON

Cover by Dugan Design Group, Bloomington, Minnesota

Cover photo © Petinov Sergey Mihilovich / Shutterstock

Published in association with the Books & Such Management, 52 Mission Circle, Suite 122, PMB 170, Santa Rosa, CA 95409-5370, www.booksandsuch.com.

CLUTTER FREE
Copyright © 2015 by Kathi Lipp
Published by Harvest House Publishers
Eugene, Oregon 97402
www.harvesthousepublishers.com

Library of Congress Cataloging-in-Publication Data
    Lipp, Kathi
    Clutter free / Kathi Lipp.
        pages cm
    ISBN 978-0-7369-5913-1 (pbk.)
    ISBN 978-0-7369-5914-8 (eBook)
    1. Storage in the home. 2. Orderliness. 3. House cleaning. I. Title.
    TX309.L5545 2015
    648'.5—dc23

                                                            2014032371

For Dad

Acknowledgments

Great thanks go to Erin MacPherson, who kept me together. Duct tape and chewing gum, baby.

Thanks, Cheri Gregory, for sharing your stories and baring your soul when it comes to clutter.

Thanks to Amanda, Jeremy, Justen, and Kimber. You've lived this. And yet you still love me. Amazing.

Susy Flory, Renee Swope, Michele Cushatt, and Crystal Paine. God bless each of you. So thankful. So, so thankful.

So much thanks goes to my team: Kim Nowlin, Angela Bouma, Wendy Doyle, and Julie Johnson. I can't even. Love each of you godly, talented women.

Thanks go to Rod Morris, the most patient man alive, and to Rachelle Gardner, agent of the century.

To our families: the Richersons, the Lipps, and the Dobsons. Thanks for giving us the best stories.

And finally to Roger. This has been the hardest year of our lives together, and yet every day you still get up, make the bed, and remind me that you'd do it all over again.

Contents

Introduction

Clutter's Last Stand

Cheri Gregory is one of my best friends.

We are both authors and speakers. Beyond that, we have almost nothing in common.

She is working toward her doctorate in leadership. My parents wanted to throw a big party for me when I graduated from high school (I think they knew early on that was the only graduation they were ever going to see out of me).

Cheri could be happy writing all day long. I love writing. But only when I have a brilliant idea and the words to express it with (so about every three months).

Cheri doesn't watch TV. I don't understand that concept. Some of my best friends are reality stars. We haven't met, but I can tell you deep and personal stories about most of the winners of *Top Chef* and *So You Think You Can Dance*...

Cheri loves research. Enough said.

But the one other thing Cheri and I have in common, are "sisters-from-another-mister" soul mates on, is our constant battle over clutter. As we've worked together on books and speaking projects, blog posts and consulting, somehow our conversation always, always circles back to clutter.

While Cheri tends toward being a historian of clutter (she wants to keep everything that her children have ever doodled on), I am more of an overall curator of stuff. I labor under the illusion that if I just had the right pair of cream wedge sandals, all my outfits would suddenly look amazing, the right color Post-it note will help me finally become organized, and the right eye cream will change my life.

But we've both discovered that we do better with less stuff.

The good news? We are so much better off than even five years ago.

The other news? It is still something we work on every single day.

So whenever we make a new step in our personal clutter-free journey, any time there is an aha!, we share it with each other. We discuss it and dissect it and figure out how to not let a poor decision happen again (or at least not as often). And in the past several years, as our understanding of the root causes of clutter increases, the piles decrease.

As we've discussed the clutter, talked about the reasons and feelings buried underneath all that stuff, we have come to some surprising (to us) understandings of why we have allowed all these things into our lives, and more importantly, how to deal with all that clutter so it no longer rules our lives.

Our findings have fallen into three areas:

1. *The Why of Clutter*—So often, we buy in order to become, and this state of our heart has led to collecting clutter.

2. *The What of Clutter*—Our so-called logical thinking gets in the way of us getting rid of all the stuff we've collected over the years.

3. *The How of Clutter*—This is where we get to the nitty-gritty of what to do about all the clutter.

Now if you're anything like me, your temptation will be to skip to the "how" part. "Just tell me what to do with all this stuff!" you cry.

I get it. You're desperate.

But unless you deal with the heart and head issues behind your clutter, you will not be prepared to make the hard decisions to get yourself out of the mountain of things weighing you down.

And here's the secret no one ever told me—once you deal with the why, once you get to the core of why you buy and keep things you do not love and do not need, the how part becomes much easier.

Once you get the why figured out, getting rid of clutter will not only become easy, it will become joyful. I'm not kidding. When you start to see things leave your house, you will feel lighter and will want that feeling to go on and on. You will develop a disdain for anything that is not loved or needed. You will walk through a store and not want anything on the shelves because, really, you are satisfied. Yes, you may go shopping to purchase a new pair of sandals because yours are worn out, but you won't buy them in every color, and you won't come home with a shirt and skirt to match—because you are satisfied.

This is where I live now.

Yes, I still have my clutter battles, but they've been downgraded from clutter wars. And I want you to join me on the less cluttered side of life.

I am here to tell you my stories, along with a few from Cheri and other friends, and to play the good cop/bad cop of your clutter crimes.

Cheri tells me that I'm the cheerleader who says, "You can do it!" and "Look at how awesome your life could be if you did this one simple thing!" and she's the one who says, "Here's what you need to stop doing," and "Here's a truth that's going to hurt, but you'll be better for it."

Both of these are useful approaches when it comes to dealing with clutter. Sometimes you need the tricks and tips that will get you up and motivated. You need someone to tell you that yes, this is possible, others have gone before you, and you will survive. You need someone to give you a vision for what your life can be after the clutter is cleared.

I don't want to overlook the fact that clearing out stuff is hard work—both physically and emotionally. You need someone who is going to remind you of all the benefits of living in a clutter-free home. "Wow—look at all the peace that's waiting for you on the other side of that stack of *Oprah* magazines! Look how much better life is when you can find clean underwear every day. Isn't it amazing when you don't have to move piles of mail in order to fix a sandwich?"

But we need balance. We need to be reminded of the things we need to stop doing.

One of Cheri's favorite video clips is a MADtv skit where Bob Newhart is a therapist and his only piece of advice consists of two words: "Stop it." Cheri has spent a lot of time in self-reflection and God-reflection figuring out the things she just had to stop doing. Sadly, having Bob Newhart yelling "Stop it!" at you is not all that is required.

Cheri is also, with a lot of love, a truth-teller. (Someone who tells you the truth with love? That's a friend. Someone who just tells you the truth? That's a jerk.) She discovers hard truths about herself and then changes old behaviors. And because she and I are seeking the same answers, she shares them with me. It's the hard work of change, but it's the lasting work of change.

I've also asked my author friend Erin MacPherson to jump in on the discussion to talk about the reality of clutter in the midst of family life. She's living the clutter battle as she raises three kids, all preschool and elementary ages, and she has real advice to share in the midst of Legos and Barbie accessories.

So realize that the advice in this book is not coming from women who have never struggled. We will be open and candid with you about our clutter journeys, not to show you how far we've come but to show you how close you are to the good stuff that lies beyond the piles.

And we'll also give you the honest, this-will-work truth and advice you need to cut the clutter and regain a foothold into a simple, meaningful, and less-stressed life.

And the one thing that all of us would tell you? When it comes to dealing with your stuff, peace is possible.

You can do this.

Part 1

Uncovering the Costs of Clutter

1

Why Your Home Is Cluttered

Yes, there are lazy people out there who simply watch TV instead of dealing with the clutter around them. But I'm guessing that's not you. If you've picked up a book to help you deal with your clutter, I can pretty much guarantee your issue is not laziness.

But knowing we aren't lazy about the situation and fixing the situation are two different things.

By *clutter* I mean anything that is in your house that hasn't earned the right to be there, or it has earned the right, but hasn't found its permanent home.

As I drilled down on my own clutter issues, and discussed it with others who have struggled with the same, I began to recognize patterns that emerge in most of us. Some of these I was totally unconscious of until I started to not just work on my clutter but to look more closely at the real reasons behind my clutter.

What I discovered are nine everyday actions that were causing my clutter. If you recognize these in yourself (and I suspect you will), be encouraged that I offer solutions for each of these throughout the book. Once you're aware of the problem, it is so much easier to deal with it.

And so much more productive than walking around your house muttering, "Why can't I just get my life together?"

Everyday Actions that Cause Clutter

You rearrange clutter instead of dealing with it.

Whenever you store something, pile it up, put it down "just for a minute," buy a tub to put it in, or shove it into a closet or drawer to deal with it "when there's more time," you are simply playing musical chairs with your stuff instead of really dealing with it.

And who can blame you? Life is busy and you have so much stuff to deal with.

But when you do take the time to really deal with your stuff, by either putting it where it needs to go or giving it away, it frees up space on all the surfaces in your home and brings peace.

You don't have an easy way to put away the things that matter.

When every time you want to put your yoga pants away in your drawer, but first you have to squeeze down the piles of unworn sweats, concert T-shirts from the nineties, and the bicycle shorts you wore exactly once, it suddenly becomes physically painful to put away laundry.

When all your "put away places" are bursting at the seams, you will stop putting things away. It's just too much hassle. Herein lies the reason most people don't mind doing laundry until it comes to putting it away. Putting it away is the painful part because it requires an overhaul on every drawer you open.

You have no routine.

Are you reinventing your systems every time you come into the house? For those of us who are prone to clutter, routine is hard. It feels boring and stifling, and if you're like me, it's hard to stick to because it always feels like there must be a better way.

But if you can start to incorporate even a little routine into your life, it will get you so much closer to the clutter-free existence you long for. A routine might be as simple as, "Every time I bring in the mail, I put it in the box next to my computer," or "Every time I buy a new piece of clothing, I donate two until there's space in my closet."

Start to take note of your clutter trail each day. Probably you are doing productive things, but not in a productive way:

- You wash, dry, and fold laundry, but then don't put it away.

- School papers go in a new place each day.

- You don't know what to do with a receipt, so you put it on the fridge with a magnet.

You are not aware—until a crisis hits.

It may be that we have friends coming over for dinner. Suddenly, everywhere I look it's as if wild hyenas ran through my house and left destruction in their wake. Sadly, there are no hyenas. Only me and my people.

For some of us who struggle with organization, we can truly appreciate the mess only when outside forces poke on our world. Then we start to see what a pit we've created for ourselves.

You have no reliable way of finding the things you put away.

If you are anything like me, you are reluctant to put things away because for you, "Out of sight is out of mind." So you leave everything important on your desk or on the kitchen counter. The problem with that? When everything is important, nothing stands out, so nothing is important.

This is why Reliable Retrieval Systems are so important. Some of my Reliable Retrieval Systems are:

- My tickler file for all my papers, instead of just piling them on my desk. I explain this in *The Get Yourself Organized Project*, and I also describe that system here in appendix 2.

- My email filing system for any correspondence I need to get back to (instead of all my email being in my inbox overwhelming me).

- A bookshelf dedicated to books I need to read (instead of stacking them up on my nightstand and desk).

- One binder for all the recipes I've printed off the Internet and have actually tried and liked (instead of all of them being stuck to my refrigerator by a dozen magnets).

You don't know where things should go.

You grew up in a house that was in constant chaos, so you never learned where things should go. Your mother-in-law's house is the picture of order, but when you try to duplicate her methods in your home, it doesn't seem to translate. You may not have enough confidence in yourself to make the decisions that need to be made about where things go.

You don't know the value of what you have.

When you're overwhelmed, it's easy to shove things into a bag or a box to sort through later. So you shove everything on the desk into a shoebox and hide that box out of sight. The problem comes when you're looking for the receipt you need to turn in, and it may be in that box, but who knows? It's mixed up with a week's (or a month's) worth of junk mail, bills, and a Happy Meal toy. It's so much to go through, it's just easier to put it off.

When you save everything, you can find nothing.

You are stuck in indecision.

You don't know where something goes, so instead of forcing yourself into a decision, you put off deciding. This leads to piles of decisions that need to be made. And when is a good time to deal with that? Never.

You punish yourself with your past mistakes.

Sometimes, instead of getting rid of something that turned out to be a not-so-great purchase (maybe the protein shake that tastes like someone took a handful of chalk and some pencil shavings and ground them up in your smoothie maker?), you hold on to them because it cost so much or it took so long to find, you think you need to just suck it up and use it. Why are you punishing yourself keeping what you don't need?

Each of these nine reasons is addressed in the pages of this book. Was it frustrating to see how many of these are why you are constantly dealing with clutter? Well, take heart. These aren't just your clutter causes—they are everyone's. And they can be overcome.

Yes, they still rear their ugly heads in my life. But I have a plan to deal with all of them. And I'm sharing that plan with you in the pages to come.

2

Finding Contentment with Living Small

The world tells you that you need to go bigger.

A bigger house, a bigger closet to hold your bigger wardrobe, a bigger car (yes, you need a minivan right this minute if you have one child—who is two). In order to be happy, you must supersize your life.

And without realizing we have bought into go-bigger thinking, we have. Big time.

"Someday, I want to have a grownup house."

I could understand the weight behind these words my husband spoke without any further explanation from him.

Oh, we had a house. Or more to the point, we were in a long-term relationship with our bank over this house. But we lived in a tiny condo—thirteen hundred square feet. When the average American house is twenty-six hundred square feet, you get an idea why Roger wanted a little more elbow room.

Oh, and we had three full-sized teenagers living with us.

And we both worked from home at least 50 percent of the time. We were bursting at the suburban seams.

On top of that, we had just combined households, and our

super-pared-down stuff was still taking over our lives. So I understood, deep within my bones, Roger's desire to have more space.

So we planned and dreamed of the bigger house we could get. Yes, it would mean Roger would have to commute an extra hour or two on the days he went in to work. Yes, we would be moving farther away from our church and our support network. But what's a family to do when there is just no room?

We live in San Jose, California, which *Forbes* ranks number four among The Most Overpriced Cities in America. (Swell.) It was not a great time to be looking to buy a new home. But the real deciding factor was our kids.

Both Roger's ex-wife and my ex-husband lived locally. If we moved out of town, our kids would either see their other parent less often (not something we wanted to do to them) or possibly go to live with that other parent and we would see them less often (not something we wanted to do to ourselves). So our best plan was to try to make the current house work.

At about the same time, I started to become fascinated with simple living and the Tiny House Movement (because I become obsessed with weird things like make-your-own-cheese kits, container gardening, and Tiny Houses). A Tiny House is typically between one hundred square feet and four hundred square feet in size. The main purposes in living tiny are to save on housing costs, to be kind to the environment, and mobility (many are built on wheels). These are all motivated by a call to a simpler life.

While we didn't feel the need to move into a Tiny House (mostly that's for singles and couples, not two parents and their three adult-sized kids), we did begin to see the possibilities that could make life work with our "if not tiny then smallish" house.

For so long, our dream had been to have a bigger home. And now we do—not because we moved into a bigger space, but because we have less stuff in the same space.

Now before you think I'm advocating that you build a 375-square-foot shack in the woods, let me be clear: You probably don't need a smaller house. My question to you is, do you really need a bigger house? Or is there a way to be content with the space you have?

And many of you don't have a choice to go bigger. So there is value in making your current space work.

I will tell you, purposely living smaller is a hard concept to wrap your mind around. Instead of thinking, *How do we earn more so we can buy a bigger house?* your thoughts must turn to, *How do we get rid of more so we can enjoy the house we're in?* Or even, *How do we pare down so we can move into a smaller house and get out from under this overwhelming debt?*

Here are some of our favorite reasons for choosing to stay in our small home:

- Smaller houses are generally less expensive to own compared to larger houses in the same neighborhood.

- Smaller houses are less expensive to furnish than larger houses.

- Smaller houses are less expensive to heat and cool compared to comparably built larger homes.

- Smaller houses force you to use all of your home. When I lived in a larger home, I rarely used our backyard. In our smaller home, we use our back patio as a second living room. We take our books outside to read, our computers outside to work, and our plates outside to eat.

- Smaller houses force you to be intentional about your possessions. You can't just keep collecting stuff without there being consequences. Either you will start feeling cluttered or (heaven forbid) you'll rent a storage unit so you don't have to deal with it.

- Smaller houses force family time. OK, this is not an advantage every single day, but it is most of the time.

- Smaller houses are easier to clean (this may be my favorite reason of all).

- Smaller houses (and the parents who live in them) teach our kids that more isn't more.

- Smaller houses give back to us with reclaimed time, energy, and money that we can then put into the values we cherish.

There are many, many advantages to smallish-house living, and even if you live in a real-sized house, understanding and embracing these ideas will help you become radically more content in the space you're already in. And I'm the last one to suggest that you give up your normal-sized house and move to a four hundred square footer with your two kids and a dog.

But where our minds usually go (at least for me and my husband) is that in order for us to be happier, we need to go bigger. We need more room so we aren't on top of each other all the time. We need an extra room for guests. We both need offices to work out of.

With advances in technology, a lot of those needs are no longer true:

- I have a laptop, so 90 percent of my office work can be done in any room of the house.

- We have an Aerobed we can inflate when we have company, so we don't need a dedicated guest room.

- With so many of us not watching TV on actual TVs anymore, we no longer need a dedicated TV room.

- With a home business, I used to need a ton of storage space for files. Now I keep them "in the cloud" and can get rid of 90 percent of my paper storage.

Learning to Be Content with the Home You Have

So instead of longing for that bigger home, how do you become content with the home you already have?

Realize the awesome power of clearing the clutter.

Every broken toy you throw out, every extra mug you donate, every kid bike you bring to a shelter, you are gaining back square feet in your home. You are clearing the clutter to a bigger home. Instead of the hassle of moving all your clutter to a bigger space (in order to accumulate more clutter), you are reclaiming your own home without spending an extra dollar to do so.

Look at how you're using your home.

Is your space and your stuff a reflection of who you are and who you want to be? Is the clutter choking out your space, time, energy, and money?

Have around only those things that have earned the right to be there.

We will talk more about this in the chapter titled "A New Approach to Cleaning Clutter," but when you see in your home only those things that you use, love, and would be willing to purchase again, your home becomes a place of refuge instead of a cacophony of visual noise.

Return to your past love.

Remember when you moved into your current space? You had visions of how your home was going to look: the walls you were going to paint, the art you were going to hang, the treasures you were going to display. And then life happened, and with life comes clutter. And clutter is the thief of creativity. Eventually, your space seems depressing, small, and joyless.

But take heart—when you finally clear the space, you will fall in love with your home all over again.

Small is good. Let's take that time you used to work harder to earn more money so you could live in a larger space and put it toward living in (and loving) the space you're already in.

3

The Spiritual Side of Clutter

The comments. Oh, the comments.

"I picked up this book to help with organizing, and in the first chapter there are Bible verses?"

"Yeah, I don't really see what religion has to do with organizing."

Those are just a couple of comments that people posted around the web about my book, *The Get Yourself Organized Project*. (Nothing like posting bad reviews of your previous book in your new book to instill confidence in your reader.)

But I stand by my book. Because I think our spirit and our stuff are linked in a multitude of ways.

There are a couple of types of clutter. There's the everyday clutter that comes with living life, raising kids, and getting things done. This clutter usually gets handled every couple of days, and your house gets back to normal. We all have that clutter, and it's just part of life.

But for some of us, clutter can go much deeper. It's the piles of bills that aren't dealt with, the stacks of unopened mail, the bags of purchases that need to be returned but won't be. It's the laundry that's ignored and the piled up dishes. It's regularly not being able to find your checkbook or your child's schoolbooks.

And yes, there is a spiritual side to that.

Because what I'm describing right there? That's a lack of peace.

My husband has often said that he wants our house to be clean enough to feel safe but cluttered enough to feel loved. I think the best way to determine the right balance is to figure out when your house becomes a blessing or a burden.

When my house is so messy and cluttered that I don't want to do the things I believe God has called me to (loving my family, working, preparing meals, spending time with him), then there's a problem. On the other hand, when I'm spending so much of my time making sure my home is perfect that I don't have time for those things God has called me to, that's a problem as well.

There is a spiritual sweet spot to our stuff.

This is not going to look the same for everyone. Each of us has to determine that for herself. But I want you to experience peace.

I want you to make a meal without feeling like you need to gut the kitchen first.

I want you to sit down and read your Bible to get spiritually fed without being distracted by all the piles screaming at you for attention the entire time.

I want you to play a game with your kids without first having to tell them, "We'll do it after I clean the house."

I want you to be able to focus on what really matters instead of focusing on, well, what doesn't.

And I want you to have the peace—spiritually and emotionally—to be the person God created you to be. Here are some of the ways that clutter and spirituality go hand in hand.

High Clutter Means High Stress

Researchers at UCLA's Center on the Everyday Lives of Families (CELF) found a link between high cortisol (stress hormone) levels in female home owners and a high density of household objects. In other words, the more stuff, the more stress women feel.

And every woman on the planet said simultaneously, "Duh."

It's not a surprise to any of us: the more stuff, the more stress. And that's why our stuff battle is a spiritual battle.

Many of you are out in the world, working a full-time job, and then come home to an overstuffed house and an overstressed life. Others of you are home all day with little kids, trying to stem the tide of stuff as you raise these little humans and feeling stressed and anxious the entire time.

Our stuff stresses us out.

But friends, this is the very thing that can give us hope. We've tended to view our messy house as a lack of discipline, a reason to be mad at ourselves, but really, the battle is bigger than that.

I think of it this way. Before a surgeon takes a scalpel to a patient to save their life, the surgical team first must make sure the operating room and everything in it are scrubbed down and sanitary. I think in similar ways this applies to our homes and lives. In order to do the life-giving work we've been called to, we must have a clean surface to work on.

Satan uses a lot of things to distract us. And most of the time, it's not bad stuff. Eating food is not bad, until we eat too much of it. Having clothes is a gift, until we can't get dressed in the morning because we have too many choices. Kids' toys are a blessing, until they start to look like a pile of junk because there are too many.

Not only is our stuff causing us stress, it's also a measuring stick of our spiritual lives.

The Pleasure and Privilege of Non-Ownership

Several years ago, Roger said, "Would you do me a favor and write a best seller so we could buy a cabin in the woods?"

My response? "Yeah, I've been holding back so far. But now that you asked, I'll get right on that."

It was a funny request, but I understood the heart behind it. Roger works very hard as an engineer here in the Silicon Valley, but his heart is in nature. He loves hiking or sitting around a campfire. He loves being surrounded by trees and the great outdoors. So any time we have the chance to go to the woods, we are there.

But wouldn't it be so much better if we owned a house where we could escape to whenever the nature urge hit? A place we could call our own?

A couple of weeks later, my friend Sharon (who did have a book on the *New York Times* best-sellers list) called to let me know that she and her husband had just bought a cabin in the woods.

Sharon had received a royalty check from the book, and her husband had some stocks that were optioned. They were not in the market for a house, but had been driving past this one and saw the real estate agent's sign. When they called to inquire about the house, the agent quoted a price and then said, "Yeah, it's not even on the market yet. They are really looking to sell. I bet they would take less for it," and then mentioned a price that was 20 percent less than the original. Sharon and her husband were sold.

The great news? Sharon told us we could use the cabin whenever she and her husband weren't using it. (I've changed her name to protect her from inquiries from other friends.)

Now part of me was happy for her. She and her husband are both hard workers and love the outdoors as much as Roger does. All of their hard work was paying off.

But I have to admit a part of me was jealous. Jealous that they owned a cabin. I know that seems selfish and petty (after all, we could use their cabin just about whenever we wanted!), but something deep inside of me wanted to own that cabin. *Own* it.

So we would go up to the cabin, grateful but also longing. Longing to own our own cabin in the woods.

Isn't that what we do? That's why the best time to sell someone a timeshare is when they are on vacation. Even if it costs more than we would ever spend on our average family getaway, there is something about owning a place (even if it's only for one week a year) that cuts to the heart of who we are. We want to own, acquire, and rule over our stuff.

But Roger and I discovered something over the years of using the cabin: not owning something rocks!

Whenever I talk to Sharon on the phone, she's telling me about some improvement that she and her husband are making on the cabin. They are putting in a tankless water heater as I write these sentences. Sharon asked us to grab the deck furniture and BBQ out of the garage when we go up there in a week because they had just stained all the woodwork.

You know what Roger and I do when we go to the cabin? We will take hot baths with water from the new heater, and cook dinner on the recently stained deck. Sharon's husband loves making improvements to the property. Roger and I simply enjoy the property.

Oh sure, we try to pitch in. Roger, being an engineer, has upgraded their wireless network (he's a handyman for the twenty-first century), and we always have the place professionally cleaned. And we always bring a gift of some toilet paper and other consumables. We have offered to pay for our time there on numerous occasions.

But I believe, with everything that is in me, that part of the reason Sharon and her husband got such a great deal on the cabin is that they have the skills and the heart to use it to bless so many other people. She says that when they bought the place, it wasn't on their mind to figure out how others could use it. But that's just who they are.

God has entrusted some things to us. I believe we are to use those things to not just bless our family but those around us as well.

Then there are things that we are not supposed to own. I was talking about buying some extra chairs to have on hand for when dinner guests come over, and my neighbor, Diane, asked why. She had a couple of folding chairs that we were welcome to borrow anytime. At first, I resisted. Something deep inside of me wants to own, wants to possess. But is owning more really an option for someone who radically needs to declutter their life?

Diane and I have keys to each other's homes. If she's out of town, I may go over and fill up her hummingbird feeder, but also may pick up a couple of chairs. And she will come over and feed our cats when we're out of town overnight, but she may also fax a document to her accountant from our all-in-one printer.

This is one of the best ways to get to know your neighbors. In the *Tightwad Gazette*, Amy calls it "Mutual Mooching." Diane and I do this all the time. I've borrowed chairs, pans, her oven on Thanksgiving, and even her house when she was out of town and Roger and I had a friend spend the night. Diane has borrowed extra outdoor chairs, ingredients, and Roger will throw on a burger for her when we're grilling.

When it comes to mutual mooching, the best way to start is by offering something of yours. I tend to do this with people I love, not because I want something in return, but because I love when I can see the resources I have being used by others. Roger and I do this with games, technology, and even cars when the need arises. There are other people out there who are eager to do the same. They love being good stewards of the space, time, energy, and money they have been entrusted with.

When you find these people, you suddenly know you don't need to own every Disney movie because the Thompsons down the road have them all, and you can borrow one anytime. But the Thompsons know to check with you before buying a board game because your family has a great collection. Owning things we use and love is great. Multiplying their use and usefulness is rewarding.

Other Benefits of Non-Ownership

When we can get past our need to own, it can have a bevy of other benefits.

Opens relationships

Author and speaker Nigel Marsh says, "There are thousands and thousands of people out there leading lives of quiet, screaming desperation, where they work long, hard hours, at jobs they hate to enable them to buy things they don't need to impress people they don't like."

When we spend all of our time working to acquire clutter, organizing clutter, and then working to pay for bigger houses to house all that clutter, it steals us away from the relationships in our lives. Clutter keeps us from connecting with those we love.

But non-ownership? That forces us to forge better and deeper relationships. I know Sharon and her husband better because of our shared connection over their cabin. My neighbor and I are closer because of our sharing of stuff. And parents of adult children can tell you the power of a working washing machine to get your kids to spend more time at your home.

Opens homes

While the rest of the world is telling you all their organizing tricks, here is the best one: own less stuff.

Owning less stuff is the key to everything. And when your home is more open, you are more willing to open your home to others.

Clutter builds a barrier between you and the rest of the world. But when the clutter is cleared, you have more space for everything— activities you love, people you love.

Frees up money

Not only do you have to pay for stuff, you have to pay to store that stuff and repair that stuff. How much money goes into just maintaining our stuff? We buy stuff in order to save time, to make us more productive, but in the end, it's the time that we spend managing, maintaining, and moving that stuff that robs us of our time and joy.

Frees up energy

When you have to move possessions in order to work or cook dinner, life is a little more exhausting.

Gives us time

Wouldn't it be nice if every weekend of your life wasn't dedicated to moving stuff around? Every thing we bring into our homes costs us time, even some of those "time-saving" devices.

I wonder how many opportunities have been missed, how many adventures have been passed over, how many relations have been strained because we've had to consider the mountains of stuff?

If you were offered a great job in a new community, how heavy would the thought of moving your possessions factor into your decision?

I think one of the greatest gifts a clutter-free life can give us is the opportunity to follow God wherever he leads. Jesus tells us exactly how to live a life that is closer to God: "Jesus said to [the rich young man], 'If you wish to be complete, go and sell your possessions and give to the poor, and you will have treasure in heaven; and come, follow Me'" (Matthew 19:21 NASB).

What this means to me, when it comes to clutter, is this:

1. *Walk lightly.* Have as few things as possible in your possession.

2. *Give what you have*, both financially and materially, to the poor.

3. *Follow God.* You will not be encumbered by stuff, so you can follow God wherever he leads.

The world wants to tell you that freedom can be bought in a car that can take you anywhere, in convenience food that will save ten minutes of prep, in electric scissors (which if you are a quilter, I get; otherwise no), and in "self-cleaning" shower electronic spray.

So here are a few questions about what things should you own and what could you let others own for you:

- Do you need to own skis when you go to the snow only every three years, or could you rent the equipment when you get there?

- Do you need to own a sewing machine that you use only to make costumes every other year, or could you borrow a friend's for this need?

- Do you need to own a weed whacker, or could you and a neighbor share?

- How about the new John Grisham best seller? Do you need to buy that today, or could you wait until your friend is done with hers or the library eventually has copies to check out?

- Must you own that fondue pot? Or could you borrow your mom's for your annual Melting Pot Party?

Owning is not bad. But we must understand that there is a price to be paid for everything we own. Owning too much chips away at our freedom.

But freedom is the knowledge that you have what you need, what you love, and you have resources to care for those that God points you to and can follow him wherever he takes you.

Quite simply, every piece of clutter I give away gets me closer to the life I'm designed to live. One of peace. One of freedom.

4

Recognizing the Real Cost of Clutter
(or How I Accidentally Had 12 Bookcases)

Organizational systems are to cluttered homes what credit cards are to debt. Credit cards tell you there is still more money, even though your bank account says no. Organizational systems tell us there is still more space, when our house cries "No!"

"You can have it all, you just have to organize it better." We tell ourselves that we can organize our stuff later, so go ahead and get that "one more thing."

We are a country addicted to our freedom—our "freedom to have." We want to have everything, pay nothing, and never feel the effects of having too much stuff.

Let's look at the book that someone just gave me. Innocently, I took the book home, thinking, *This book will take up less than an inch of horizontal space on my bookshelf. What's the harm?*

But what I forget about are the dozens of other books that take up an inch or so on those shelves. When I combine those inches, I am now looking at shelves that need to be managed. And then shelves become entire pieces of furniture that now need to be housed somewhere in my living space.

What Clutter Costs Us

Every single item coming into our home costs us something:

It costs us space.

It you are truly battling clutter, you know this is a biggie.

Going back to that book.

I was raised by a mom who didn't read and didn't swim (not that she couldn't read, but it wasn't something she enjoyed). She was determined that her kids would turn out differently. So early on, she enrolled both my brother and me in our library's reading program and in swimming lessons. Her plan worked—for the most part. My brother lied to the swim instructor on the first day and told her, "My mom said I couldn't get my head wet." I became a voracious reader and a competitive synchronized swimmer. (Mock all you want. I want to see you lift another girl straight out of the water with no help except Amazonian-like legs kicking furiously underwater.)

So it's been very hard to wrap my head around the concept that one could ever have enough books.

But let me assure you. One can.

I have to admit that I collect books like little trophies. If I read and appreciate a book, it shows what a clever, deep thinking person I am. (OK, so maybe my collection of *Calvin and Hobbes* books is not truly indicative of deep thinking, but I keep those on the bottom shelf.) I like having books around me. Especially my favorites.

So I just kept collecting and collecting, adding bookshelves around the house to display my ever-expanding library. Until I had twelve bookcases: two bookshelves in each of the kids' rooms (four total), one in the hall, two in our bedroom, two in the kitchen, two in the living room, and one in the bathroom (what were we thinking?).

Twelve bookshelves.

It totally snuck up on us.

And we were running out of space in those as well. Between buying books I want, getting books from friends and publishers, and getting books at conferences, we were exploding books throughout the house. And it was crazy. For several reasons:

- I hadn't read maybe half the books that were "mine" (as opposed to kid books or the hubby's books).

- I had no criteria for what to do with a book when I was done reading it.

- It never occurred to me that I should ever get rid of a book. That would have been the same as getting rid of family heirlooms or pictures.

I had to change the way I thought about books.

We now have three bookcases (one for general reading, one for my work books, and one for Roger's work books) and a shelf of cooking, home improvement, and decorating books in our kitchen.

That is after gifting several hundred (over a thousand?) books in a two-year span. Even now, my criteria for what stays on my shelves becomes stiffer and stiffer.

I am buying fewer books, reading all the ones I buy, and then doing one of three things with them:

- keep the ones I know I will read again (mostly business books or cooking, home improvement, and decorating books)

- give books away to friends, kids, or blog readers who I know would enjoy them

- donate the rest to an appropriate organization (school, library, charity)

It costs us time.

When I bring home a new egg slicer from the store, all I think about is how much time that kitchen gadget is going to save me from the laborious task of slicing all those eggs. (Probably a total of six minutes a year.) But what I don't factor in is the "time cost" of that egg slicer:

- the time it took me (or my husband) to earn the money to buy it
- the time I spent shopping for it
- the time I will spend hunting for it the three times a year I want to use it
- the time I spend moving it out of the way when I want to find another gadget and have to dig through all the other time-saving devices

Now take an item that may be a little more time consuming than an egg slicer—some piece of technology—and our time commitment goes up.

Just the caring for, storing, and clutter of too much stuff can cost us time in a hundred moments a day.

Think about all the places where your life feels cluttered: your sock drawer, your makeup counter, your closet. Now look at all the things that are cluttering it up—you are having to dig through piles of unused stuff to get to the good stuff. It's time to get rid of some of those layers and stop costing yourself time every single morning as you get ready to meet the world.

It costs us attention.

Why is your desk covered in Post-it notes, pieces of paper, folders, and workbooks? For many of us, it's because we are afraid.

If I put something away, I'll forget about it, and then something important will not get done. We use our physical world as a visual to-do list. The problem is, when there are too many visual reminders, that's called clutter, and we can't concentrate on anything.

We have to limit our visual cues to just a few select ones. Not everything can be extremely important.

It costs us energy.

And I'm not just talking physical energy. Let's consider the emotional energy that clutter steals from us. If the number one topic that creates disagreements in homes is finances, I'm guessing that clutter has to be at least a top five issue. Whether it's between spouses or parents and kids, I suspect at least 20 percent of stressful conversations in most families comes from clutter.

"I'm not going to ask you again—pick up your toys!"

"Can't you put your clothes in the hamper like the rest of the world?"

"I need you to help me clean up before your parents get here. *Now!*"

And when the clutter level is raised in your home, it naturally raises the stress level. So when you're searching for and can't find the right notebook for your son's astronomy class or a stamp to mail your mother-in-law's birthday card, it turns a normal conversation into a stressed-out conversation. No wonder we're dying to get to the weekend, only to realize that sometimes it's easier to be out of the house than to deal with the people and the clutter surrounding us.

At some points in this book, I'm going to ask you to do some extraordinary things. I'm going to ask you to make some hard choices when it comes to your clutter. When I do, remember what that clutter is costing you. When I ask you to get rid of something that cost you five dollars (or fifty dollars), think about the cost you're really paying by holding on to that item.

Part 2

Why We Buy Stuff

5

Why We Buy

Why do we buy what we don't want and don't need?

About seven years ago, Roger and I traveled to the Atlanta area to see his family. Now let me start off by saying I love Roger's family. No—I adore them. But can we all agree that sometimes, even in the best of families, staying at other people's homes can be a wee bit stressful?

Some family members were frustrated with us because we slept late. (We were on California time, so our "sleeping late" was getting up at five in the morning according to our body clocks.) Others were frustrated because we stayed with one family member and not the other. Plus there is just the interruption in routine. We were tired and worn out, and I was missing my kids who had just started their summer vacation.

Oh, and it was hot. It was summer in Atlanta, so I guess that was a given.

After spending five days with his family, Roger and I met with a business colleague and his wife. We went to the Ormewood Park area and ate at a cute, hip brunch place and did a little shopping nearby.

His wife and I went into a boutique while the boys waited outside. After being in several shops, I had the itch to buy something. And I found it. A light-green scarf with brown and cream patterns on it. It was cute. It was also $56.

Let's be clear—I've bought a lot of (too many) scarves in my life. But I can't remember a time that I've ever paid over $20. But suddenly $56 seemed like a totally reasonable amount to pay for this scarf.

So I bought it. And then I bought some Post-it notes in a stationery store. And a little stuffed bear for my daughter Kimberly. And a fancy potato peeler at a kitchen gadget store.

In other words, I lost my mind.

I don't tend to go on shopping sprees, but that day, if I wanted it, I convinced myself that I had to have it.

I wore the scarf exactly once (to prove to Roger that I loved it).

My daughter liked the bear and thanked me for it, but her look said, "Why are you giving me a bear, Mom?"

The potato peeler turned out to be just like one I already had at home that I forgot I'd bought.

The only thing I've really used? The Post-it notes.

I have looked back at that day and tried to analyze why it was such an epic fail. Here are some of the conclusions I've come to:

- I was tired and hot. I told Roger before we got married, "For your own safety, it would be smart to never let me get too tired or too hot. Or too hungry. I'm telling you this because I love you." I make stupid decisions when I'm uncomfortable. I want to do something comforting—like buy things or eat.

- I was stressed. It had been a long week with mixed expectations, and I felt I had disappointed some of Roger's family. I was stressed about it. When I'm stressed, I do things to relieve the stress. (See shopping and eating above.)

- I wanted to impress people. Why buying things I don't need to impress other people seems like a good idea, I have no idea. I wanted to appear successful to our business associate and his wife, and I thought spending my way there was a good idea. I now see people who don't needlessly spend as the ones who really have it together.

- I felt that I deserved it. After a week of being away from home and missing my kids, I felt like I deserved a treat.

The problem, of course, is that buying things we don't love or need leads us to clutter. And clutter is the opposite of where our heart should be:

> Keep your lives free from the love of money and be con-
> tent with what you have, because God has said,
>> "Never will I leave you;
>>> never will I forsake you."
>> (Hebrews 13:5)

God knows our tendency to fill our lives with stuff instead of the stuff that matters. That's why money is mentioned so often in the Bible—we have an intense relationship with money and the stuff it can buy.

But God is clear that when we surround ourselves with less stuff, we can have more of the things that matter: his presence, peace, contentment, and joy. As Paul says in his letter to the church at Philippi:

> I know what it is to be in need, and I know what it is to have plenty. I have learned the secret of being content in any and every situation, whether well fed or hungry, whether living in plenty or in want. I can do all this through him who gives me strength (Philippians 4:12-13).

Stuff is a short-term fix to a long-term longing—to have enough. The problem is what we're longing for can't be satisfied by our stuff.

6

So Really, Why Do I Keep Doing That?

O ur heart causes us to buy what we don't really need.

I spend a lot of my waking hours teaching women about themselves, their relationship to God and others. And whenever I talk about how we as women get twisted in how we see ourselves, I tell them that the world uses three things to keep us reliant, trapped, and constantly seeking answers in the products that we buy: *fear*, *guilt*, and *shame*.

Look around your house at the things you bought that you don't really need or love. Those Christmas dishes you've used exactly once. The Happy Meal toy on the kitchen counter. The shoes you bought on the way to a party. Most of those purchases can be traced back to a core feeling.

You bought the Christmas dishes because you were hosting a new group of friends for a holiday dinner, and suddenly every other dish in your house seemed, well, blah. You found these at the fourth shop you went to. They weren't your favorite—you wouldn't have bought them if you didn't have people coming over—but they were fine. Problem is, after you used them for the one party, you never loved them enough to pull them out again.

You've had a busy week and haven't been able to spend as much time playing with your kids as you like. As you're running errands, your daughter sees that McDonald's has Teenie Beanies as their Happy Meal toy. Even though it's not lunch time, you pull in and order the meal. Your daughter is thrilled to get the blue bear. But then you find it on your kitchen counter four days later, abandoned and forgotten.

You bought the shoes on the way to a friend's birthday party. You were going to see a lot of people you hadn't seen in a while, and you wanted to look just right. The shoes you were wearing were OK, but you wanted a little bit higher heel. The new shoes hurt, but it's just for one party. And you've never worn them again.

We buy the dishes out of *shame*. ("Nothing I have is good enough. I want people to think I've got it together.") Or *fear*. ("What will they think about these fifteen-year-old plates? Either they'll think that I actually like them, or we are too broke to buy the ones we like.") And the shoes? Whenever we are trying to find the "perfect" anything, that's usually shame rearing its ugly head. And we all know that *guilt* drive-by from McDonald's.

So let's go a little deeper into these three emotions that encourage us to buy.

Fear

Fear tells us, "Bad things will happen if you don't…" This is the surface level of our heart issue with clutter. Fear commands us to buy and acquire.

If I don't stock up on food, I may not have money at the end of the month to buy anything.

If I don't buy that shirt now, it will be gone when I come back for it.

If I don't buy twenty rolls of Forever stamps now, they might go up in price and then I'll have to spend so much more in the future.

If I don't buy three pairs of these shoes, I won't have them when the first ones wear out.

They are going to have this color of nail polish for only a limited time. If I don't buy it now, I'll never be able to get it again.

And the one I'm currently wrestling with as I pack for a trip to San Diego: *I need a new, cute outfit for this trip, otherwise I won't fit in.*

When I had my Tiny House experience (living in Japan), I also had my tiny paycheck experience. This was my first time living on my own, and managing money was not something I was used to. Plus, I was paid only once a month. Thirty-one days is a long time to go with no fresh infusion of cash.

Toward the end of my year there, I finally got smarter. I started to buy more food toward the beginning of the month that wouldn't go bad. In that case, it kept me from making soy soup (packets of soy sauce mixed with water and heated up) for the last three days of the month.

But at some point, I needed to deal with my stockpiling tendencies and keep only a little more on hand than I would actually need, instead of my pantry resembling a fallout shelter from the fifties.

Fear of going without can make us do (and buy) strange things. And advertisers know this. We see fear in advertising all the time:

Limited time offer!

Clearance!

Summer special!

Special item!

All of those signs play on our fear that we will miss out on the things that will improve our life. And instead of dealing with the emotions that surround that brokenness, we take the safer, comfortable route and slowly let ourselves drown in the stuff of our lives.

Guilt

Guilt tells us, "You've done bad things and now you need to make up for them…" And guilt commands us to make up for those bad things by buying and acquiring.

You decided to go to work instead of staying home with your kids? You need to make up for it by buying them more toys.

You decided to stay home with your kids instead of going to work to pay for a private education? You need to make up for it by buying them educational toys.

You didn't visit your mom on her birthday? You need to make up for it by buying her a bigger present.

Deborah Bohn, in her article "Too Many Toys!" at Babyzone.com, talks about guilt as a motivation for buying stuff we don't need:

> "I could write a book about guilt," says Tom Limbert, head teacher of Stanford University's Bing Nursery School of Child Development Research and Training. "Parents are driven so much by guilt, especially working parents and single parents. It's amazing." Limbert says that parents often buy toy after toy to appease their own feelings of remorse for not spending time with their children.

And guess what—marketers know how to exploit our guilt as a motivation to buy. Commercials show busy families coming home after work and buying fast or frozen food. Magazines have whole Christmas issues dedicated to buying gifts for everyone from your boss to the mailman. Amazon learns your buying habits so they can find out what issue you are feeling guilty about (parenting, marriage, work, relationships) and target you with their "recommended for you" items to buy. So much of what we buy—for ourselves and especially for the people we live with—is making up for what we feel we should have done or should not have done.

So what do we do? We can buy the organizing books, download the charts, and resolve to get rid of the clutter. But if we don't attack the heart of the issue—the *fear*, *guilt*, and *shame* in our lives that cause us to buy what we don't really need—we are going to use that clutter to build our own prisons and keep us from connecting with others.

But I don't need to be the one to tell you that buying doesn't lead us to feeling less guilt. In fact, all guilt buying does is leave us with tangible reminders of our attempts to assuage the guilt in the first place. Leaving us feeling more guilty.

Here are some ways that guilt buying can be turned on its head:

- Set a gift budget and stick to it creatively (for example, get your mom a "movie kit" with a movie and popcorn instead of tickets to an expensive theater).

- Reward your children with time (things like a trip to the pool or park).

- Whenever you feel like you want to give someone something, see if you can give them time instead.

Shame

Shame says, "I am defective. I need to prove to the world that I'm not."

I've told you, I'm not writing this book from a carefree, clutter-free perspective. I am someone who deals with these issues every single day of my life. So why am I qualified to write the book? Because I'm no longer huddled in a corner, rocking back and forth, because of these issues. And I can almost always find my car keys. Clutter no longer keeps me down. I deal with it and move on.

But when I'm tired or overwhelmed, it's easy for the shame of clutter (and other areas of my life) to drag me down.

I think shame is our biggest motivator to acquire stuff we don't need. Everything in our world is screaming "You are not enough. Smart enough. Pretty enough. Thin enough. Hip enough." So when I know I'm not enough, the people who produce these products promise me there's a cure for not being enough—it's their product. Their product is going to make my teeth whiter, my husband happier, and my kids better behaved.

Shame tends to rear its ugly head when:

I have company coming over. When I have someone coming over for the first time (especially if it's someone I admire or am secretly hoping to impress), I look around at my house, and suddenly everything I own looks shabby without the chic.

I have a big event I'm going to. Oh, this gets me every time. I have a big event coming in a matter of days. Wanting to look awesome, I head to the mall and look for something to wear. There is nothing awesome at the mall, so I settle on something passable. Then I get home and realize I have almost the identical outfit hanging in my closet.

I'm feeling rushed. It's the night before a big trip, and I run out to Target to buy a few things: travel shampoo, hairspray, socks. The problem? I probably have all these at home, but I'm too rushed and scattered to pull them together.

So how do you deal with the shame that's making you buy? Here's what I did once I realized that was what was happening.

When I have company coming over, I commit to enjoy instead of impress. I am on the board of directors for a regional writers' conference. After finding out where the other six board members lived, the choice of where to have our meetings became obvious: my house.

I have been in this position before where people I respect and admire were coming to my house for the first time. And I knew I had to overcome my initial impulse to buy new everything in order to make sure my house looked right. Before my clutter-free commitment, I would have gone out and bought a new tablecloth, new hand towels for the bathroom, maybe a couple of cute table decorations. I would have stressed myself out so much with making sure that everything looked right that I would not have been able to enjoy anyone's company for the first hour or so after their arrival.

So I promised myself that instead of trying to impress, my only job was to enjoy. Instead of spending time and energy running around buying things, I spent the night before making a cake (three of us on the board were celebrating our birthdays within two weeks of each other—*Cake Boss* would not have been impressed, but it tasted great) and cleaning house. I was not there to show off; I was there to invite people into my home and make sure that they felt loved and welcomed.

When I buy things to impress other people, it does nothing to build a connection. But when I do things that serve the other people—making a very unfancy cake, cleaning the bathroom, having the coffee ready as people arrive—those are all ways of serving and connecting.

And when I stop buying stuff every time someone comes over, I no longer have to deal with the fallout of all that clutter.

When I have a big event, I'm going to figure out what's already in my closet, and then iron it. When I'm feeling vulnerable because of a big event, I have to be purposeful to do noncrazy things, like looking to see what I already have that could totally work for this event. Even if I'm not crazy about anything in my closet, I at least know what I have. Now when I go to my closet, instead of declaring I have nothing to wear, I look through and try to figure out the look I'm going for and how I could accomplish it using what is already hanging there.

(A big secret I've learned? I usually have something that looks great in my closet, it just needs to be ironed. That's why I hang all my shirts that need to be ironed in another closet until there's something on TV I want to watch but feel guilty about watching it. Ironing is the guilt-free way to watch something stupid on TV.)

When I'm feeling rushed, I need to remember this feeling and give myself the gift of time. This is where planning ahead can really save you clutter (in your home and your mind). Packing the night before a trip is a killer for the woman who leans toward clutter because:

- You will over pack. Those of us who lean toward clutter never ask ourselves, "How can I make do with what I have?" No, we think of every possible scenario and pack for every contingency.

- You will not pack the right things. If I pack at the last minute, I will forget important things, like my black yoga pants. I would rather forget my toothbrush than my black yoga pants. I can get a replacement toothbrush at the front desk of almost any hotel.

- You will end up buying duplicates of stuff you already have.

As you try to stem the tide of the clutter that's coming into your home, my challenge to you is to think about the reasons you're buying. If you keep drilling down to what's causing the need to acquire, see if it's rooted in fear, guilt, or shame. If it is, deal with that *emotion* sitting in front of you instead of another *thing* you will need to deal with again later down the road.

7

Yet More Compelling Reasons to Buy Things

B ack in my early twenties I was very pregnant and very sick. My friend Kimberly came over one evening, and we were watching an old movie on TV. During one of the commercial breaks, a guy came on and started talking about how you could get rich selling real estate. Both Kim and I were pretty savvy women (for twenty-two), but by the time this infomercial was over, we were trying to decide if we could split the cost of the audio series ($199) or if we each needed our own.

Fortunately, neither of us were organized enough to send a check right then, and this was before the days of web addresses and instant buying online. The audio course that could have made us millionaires never made it into our hot, greedy little hands.

How did that guy on TV, in a matter of minutes, nearly get two intelligent-but-broke women to plop down a total of almost $400? (And before you judge us as weak-minded, have you ever wasted an hour watching a home shopping channel?) These people are masters at getting you to buy something you would never in a million years ever think you would need.

We've already talked about fear, guilt, and shame as some of the reasons we are internally motivated to buy. But there are things marketers do to play on those deep-seated emotions.

Scarcity and Exclusivity

It's amazing how quickly we can push ourselves into a decision to buy when we think that option will be taken away from us. When we see signs that say "Clearance!" or "Final Markdowns!" something in us gets triggered and we think, *I need to do this now before it all goes away.*

And that's what these TV shows are all about. They have a "limited number" of items available. Often they even have a countdown clock to increase the sense of panic.

Have you ever wondered why Starbucks doesn't serve their very popular pumpkin lattes year round? They are creating a scarcity mentality. If we could have pumpkin lattes year round, we would soon grow tired of them. But there is a social buzz heard round the world when someone spots the first sign that pumpkin lattes are here for the season. Pictures get posted on Instagram and Facebook, and the world takes a day to celebrate the return of the pumpkin. (Now that's marketing genius right there. We are doing all the advertising for Starbucks.)

Or let's take the example of the elusive Birkin bag. According to *Wikipedia,*

> Its prices range from £4,800 to £100,000 ($7,400 to $150,000). Costs escalate according to the type of materials. The bags are distributed to Hermès boutiques on unpredictable schedules and in limited quantities, creating scarcity and exclusivity.

And Robin Givhan in her *Washington Post* article, "Martha's Moneyed Bag Carries Too Much Baggage," says,

> It is virtually impossible for the typical shopper—even one brandishing a platinum American Express card or a large wad of cash—to walk into an Hermes boutique and purchase a Birkin. The bag has a waiting list that has grown

to the absurd length of 2½ years and so the French company has closed it. Now there is a wait to get on the waiting list. Unless, of course, one is a celebrity with all of the privileges that affords.

And even if you've never seen a Birkin bag, or even heard about it before now, there's a little part of most women that would suddenly like to own that bag just because it's so very hard to get.

It works with limited edition cars, and it works on clearance sales at Old Navy.

Influence

I am a book author. It is my job not just to write books, but to get them into other people's hands. And one of the best ways for me to do that is to ask people to talk about my books to their circle of influence.

Now I don't feel guilty about this in the least because my whole goal in writing is to give people hope, humor, and some practical how-tos for changing their lives for the better, and if no one reads these books, not a lot is going to change. So what do I do? I work to get people to influence buying decisions. When someone you respect recommends that you buy one of my books, you are much more likely to purchase it.

As I said, I don't feel guilty about this at all. It is my hope that you read one of my books, hang on to it to read again if you need the encouragement, use it as a daily devotional (I have some books that are set up that way), give it to a friend when you're done with it, or donate it to a library or other organization.

But when it comes to getting you to buy long-wearing, ultra-glossy, and chip-resistant nail color from Kardashian Beauty by Kourtney, Kim, and Khloe, well…that's a different story. Retailers will use anyone that you admire (the Kardashians? really?) or has influence to get you to buy what they are selling.

Influence works in a myriad of ways. It makes us feel like we belong. It makes us feel like we have an edge when it comes to trends and ideas. And for our kids, it makes them feel a little bit closer to that TV or pop star they so admire.

Selling You a Vision

One of the most powerful ways marketers get you to buy is to sell you a vision of your future if you use their product.

Your house will be 30 percent cleaner.

Your hair bouncier.

Your eyes more defined.

Your husband happier.

Your kids brighter.

When a retailer can get you to imagine what your life will be like if you use one of the products they sell, you start buying-in even before taking it to the counter. If you touch the product in the store, you are 50 percent more likely to purchase that product.

We are all smart, intelligent women. But these tactics advertisers use play on something we are all desperately looking for: hope.

That is why it's so important that we understand the reasons behind our buying. When we can recognize the gimmicks for what they are—ploys to get us to buy products—we can take a smarter look at whether a product is really going to change our lives.

So what do we do to fight back at what the advertisers are trying to sell?

Scarcity and Exclusivity vs. the Three-Day Rule. Institute a waiting period for purchases. For some it may be a day, for others it may be three days. You may need to put a price limit on it or discuss it with your husband or a friend before you purchase.

Influence vs. Limited Exposure. Grown women get caught in this trap all the time. We see someone whose sense of fashion we admire, and we long to repeat that look. If this is you (as it has been me), limited exposure to blogs, magazines, and some TV shows may be your best bet.

Vision vs. Reality. Is there really a difference between the eyeliner you want that's on display in the store and the one you have at home?

I am not a big fan of Pinterest, since I think that sometimes it can lead to needless wants and unrealistic expectations. But one thing I love it for is helping me reimagine the stuff I already have. When I look up terms like "Travel Wardrobe," I'm doing it with the intention of looking at what I already have that can be mixed up in new ways. Or putting "Denim Shirt" in the search box allows me to see new styling ideas that pop up for my old denim shirt.

When we start to recognize some of the tricks retailers are playing on us, we can start to understand when we really need or love something and when our emotions are getting the better of us. We have to be ruthless to keep new possessions out of our homes. Stop the process of acquiring before you need to spend your space, time, energy, and money on buying it, storing it, and eventually getting rid of it.

8

There's a Whole World of Better Stuff Out There...or So We Think

O ne of the lies our heart tells us: *There's a whole world of better stuff out there just waiting for you.*

Six months ago, I made one of the biggest decisions of my life. I had gastric sleeve surgery. After a lifetime of struggling with my weight, with very little success, the effects were getting hard to ignore: a consistently sore back, shortness of breath, and high blood pressure.

After a lot of prayer and some huge confirmations about the path I should take, I scheduled the surgery and waited for my day to arrive.

I would be lying if I didn't tell you that one of the reasons I was excited to have the surgery was for the clothes. I just knew that as I started to lose the weight, all those fabulous clothes that were available to the rest of the world would suddenly be mine for the taking (and a debit card, but that's another chapter). I couldn't wait until the first time I could say, "I have nothing to wear! Everything is so big." Then I'd finally have a justifiable reason to rebuild my wardrobe with all those cute clothes. Clothes from stores I hadn't been able to shop at in years.

I got rid of most of my big winter clothes after I'd lost the first twenty-five pounds, and then I hit the mall with a glint in my eye and cash burning a hole in my pocket—only to discover the sad truth that the clothes I had dreamed about and hoped for were similar to what I had before, just in smaller sizes.

Sigh.

And now I had another problem: I'd gotten rid of some great clothes. Yes, they were too big, but hiring a seamstress to take in a shirt that's appropriate for me to wear to work costs twelve dollars, and buying a new one? A whole lot more than that.

And what's even worse is the pants. Most of the pairs of pants I had so gleefully given away to Goodwill I'd already spent ten dollars to get hemmed. Now I was buying new, smaller pants and having to have those hemmed as well.

Now I know that no one is going to have sympathy for me because I'm losing too much weight to fit into my old clothes. Trust me, I'm grateful for the problem.

But like the guy who breaks up with his girlfriend instead of popping the question because he has a deep down feeling that there is certainly someone better out there, I can fall into the trap of skipping over the clothes already hanging in my closet, the food that's already in my freezer, the sheets that are already in my linen closet, because there surely is something better out there. Somewhere.

This all sounds so shallow when it's written down. I seem so weak-minded and flighty. I know that stuff doesn't make me happy, and "better" stuff doesn't make me happier. But I, like so many women who deal with clutter, have a hard time not falling into the trap.

And it's not only women who get snared by this lie. For men, often it's a better piece of sporting equipment or a new pair of sports shoes or, for my man, the latest technology. When we travel to see family, one of Roger's guilty pleasures is to try to make everyone jealous with the features on his phone. Before we started to simplify our lives, Roger was a serial upgrader: TVs, laptops, sound systems. But when you buy a new piece of technology, the cool factor wears off pretty quickly. What was awesome and envy-inducing six months ago starts to look dated.

Part of the reason we do it is to prove to the world that we are OK.

We want to feel better about the party we're going to, so we buy a new outfit to feel OK.

We want to feel better when we have people over to the house, so we buy a new tablecloth to feel OK.

So how do we shift our thinking from the desire for new and better?

It's hard. I don't know a woman who can walk through Target without feeling the urge to get a new pair of yoga pants (you know, because the old yoga pants have gotten ratty from all that relaxing) or a new spatula. And I don't know a person who can look through her house and say she truly and honestly needs every item she has in it. It's just part of our culture to have…things.

But it's also necessary to let these things go. We all know that things don't make us happy. And things will never bring us closer to God or closer to people, which is more important than having a new pair of wedges.

We all know this and agree with this, yet I think putting a clutter-free life into practice is harder than it seems. Because it's easy to let things get a grip on us.

And that's what this book is about—intentionally, purposefully, and prayerfully letting go of the things that truly don't matter so we can cling to the things that do.

A Shift in Thinking

It takes some effort and requires a significant shift in our thinking. But it is doable and I'm going to help, beginning with the following suggestions:

1. Know what you already have.

Yes, you are going to hear that a lot in this book. As we start to pare down the amount of stuff we have in our lives and keep only those things that we love and use, we will start to understand that most of what we need we already have. You probably don't really need a new and better pair of jeans—last year's are just fine.

2. Remember that, in some cases, old is better than new.

There is something really beautiful about a pair of jeans that have been perfectly worn in and fit just right. As long as they don't have holes in, say, the crotch.

3. Refurbish.

We are a throwaway society. When I told a friend that I was taking my suitcase to a repair shop, she confided that it would never, ever occur to her to repair a suitcase. I don't blame her. Shoe and luggage repair shops are becoming a thing of the past. And what if you want to repair a small appliance? You can pretty much forget about it.

And then what happens to that item that's been replaced? Somehow it hangs around our house as we think, "Well, maybe I'll get it repaired. Or maybe someone who's handy can fix it. Or maybe it will magically start working again. Or maybe my husband can fix it..." And so on and so on. And then it clutters up our house, and we can't figure out why we have so much stuff.

4. Look at your things with a different perspective.

Train your mind to see things in your house and immediately assess if they are needed. I just looked up from my computer while writing and glanced around my kitchen table. On it is a stack of paper plates (um, those can be put away), a CD I never listen to (why do I still have that?), a bottle of Gatorade (don't ask why it's not in the fridge), a cord to an electronic device I don't even recognize, and a chocolate bar (that's for me to eat while I fathom a way to deal with my cluttered kitchen). All of these things are cluttering up my space and my mind as I work, and none are necessary.

If you train your mind to immediately see things as what they are (things), then you can avoid clutter by immediately knowing where something goes. Even if it means it goes in the trash.

5. Prayerfully consider what really matters.

Last year, my friend Sandy was going through a tough time—her husband had lost his job and they were struggling to make ends meet.

They made the tough decision to sell their house, and with it they sold their furniture, their knickknacks, and 75 percent of the other things they had. Recently they moved back into a house and were thrilled with how easy packing and unpacking was. Their house is clean, neat, and organized, and they hardly miss the things they once thought they needed.

6. Think further about the possibilities.

The fact that you even picked up this book shows that you've been thinking about organization and clutter. And I want to encourage you to think even more. What will happen when you downsize and declutter? How will it affect your emotions, your mood, your family, your life? How will it affect others? How can it change your worldview and help you to become the person God intended you to be?

7. Have a heart-to-heart with your hubby.

I'm guessing that most of the stuff in your house belongs to both you and your spouse. So before you go into his man cave and donate the 1989 Oakland A's pennant to the Salvation Army, you should have a little chat with him about what you are doing and why you are doing it. Because, for the record, donating treasured sports paraphernalia is likely to set off WW III. Not that I know that from experience or anything.

8. Give yourself a new motto.

It's easy to get swept into the craziness of buying new things. (Just think of how you felt when you were, say, at Target on the day after Christmas, and you couldn't help but imagine how much you needed a new light-up singing reindeer for next Christmas's festivities.) Before you even go shopping or venture into public, remind yourself that you are a clutter-fighting superhero, and you will not be swayed by clever marketing and the nasty schemes of knickknack making corporations.

Or something like that.

Part 3

Why We Keep Stuff

9

What Your Head Tells You About Clutter

At its heart, clutter is a lack of peace.

As I write this, I'm sitting in the middle of my parents' living room surrounded by clutter. My mom would want you to know that this is not how they normally roll. But this is not a normal time in our family's life.

My dad has been in and out of hospitals over the past several months, and because of his frequenting the ER, has picked up a MRSA infection, a staph infection that is sometimes contracted in hospitals (oh, the irony). The course of action after getting the infection was for my dad to be quarantined and then placed on a two-week course of antibiotics.

Things are changing for my parents, so during this time, my mom has taken on the job of getting the downstairs (where my dad will most likely be living) ready and comfortable. She's painted the walls, getting new flooring, and rearranging things so that my dad can easily maneuver his walker in and out of his new digs.

So right now, the place is in upheaval. There is tape on the walls and picture frames on the kitchen table. Tarps cover the flat surfaces, and family treasures are out of place.

But these are the necessary evils of remaking a home. For a while, the kitchen is unusable, the living room is chaotic, and everything is out of place.

But for so many of us, this isn't the picture of one day; it's a description of every day of our lives. And that is why clutter is so harmful. It steals away the life that it promised in the first place.

When we buy that new kitchen item, it promises us a better life.

When we set something down for "just a second," it gives us the freedom to move on to something bigger and better, but it also leaves clutter in its wake.

We hold on to something we haven't used in months, maybe years, but we convince ourselves we will be able to use it again somehow, someday.

But all those things pile up, and we feel like we need a kitchen remodel before we can scramble an egg or we must first spend a day clearing out a place for a new craft project we'd love to start. Clutter does what it's so good at doing: stealing our joy.

We already know what clutter is. It's any item

- I don't use.

- I don't love.

- I wouldn't buy again.

The easiest time to say no to clutter is at the store.

The hardest time to say no to clutter is once it's crossed the threshold of your front door. Because once it comes into your home, clutter takes on a life of its own.

But another thing we must recognize about clutter is that it's active. Even if it's just sitting there on a shelf or buried in a box, clutter is actively working in our lives.

It makes us feel unsettled. Clutter never lets you rest. It is constantly talking to you and letting you know that things are wrong and there will be no peace until you tend to the mess. You cannot enjoy any activity—time with your family and friends, reading, exercising, anything, because clutter is telling you, "Pay attention to *me*!"

The problem is that clutter can become so overwhelming that to try and attack even a little of it can feel defeating. So instead, you give up and live in the piles of your own unintentional making.

Clutter never lets you settle on one thing. There is too much distraction, too much stop and start, too much "I'll get to it when I can."

It shames us. Clutter says you can't have people over, you can't celebrate birthdays or have Christmas at your house because you have too much stuff.

It steals our time. "You must pay attention to me!"

It steals our joy. "You can't have fun until you deal with me!"

It makes us exhausted. You end up having to move piles just to sit down and rest. You have to clear counters in order to make a sandwich.

It brings up bad memories. There are little emotional grenades in all of your piles, and every time you sort through one, you uncover something you "should have" done. A thank-you note that should have been written. A bill that should have been paid. A library book that should have been returned. A birthday card that should have been mailed.

It keeps you guilty. Every time you see something undone, it piles on the guilt.

But that is exactly why we need to deal with the clutter. Clutter keeps talking to us, weighing us down, and keeping us from living the life we were designed to live. Clutter is the coconspirator with our fear, shame, and guilt to keep us bogged down.

In the next several chapters, we're going to talk about how our head keeps us bogged down in clutter—the lies we tell ourselves to keep clutter alive and how we can retrain our mind to stop trusting in stuff to meet our needs.

10

Just in Case

Problem: We keep things we don't use and don't love "just in case," and then find ourselves not being able to fully function or enjoy life. Our head causes us to keep what we don't really want.

I grew up with a mom who could stretch a dollar. My dad was unemployed for much of my young life, and it was tasked to my mom to make sure that the money lasted. I remember feeling so bad for her the day I saw her wearing pieces of cardboard in her shoes to keep something between her feet and the sidewalk.

Ten years later, and I was living in Japan as a short-term missionary. I had to carefully weigh everything I brought with me, especially shoes. Without a car for transportation, I walked—a lot. And since I wear such a large size (11), there wasn't much chance of me finding a black ballet flat in my size in Japan in the nineties. So not too long after I arrived there, I developed those familiar holes, and I found just the right-sized piece of cardboard to work in the bottom of my shoes.

I vividly remember what it was like to not have enough. So for a long time afterward, I became what some might consider a shoe hoarder—just in case.

I think we're all guilty of "just-in-case" thinking from time to time. For some people, it's paperwork. ("I will hang on to every receipt for everything I've ever bought, including that pack of gum at the train station, just in case.")

For others, it's crafting items. ("No, I haven't knitted for over a decade, but maybe I will again someday. Or maybe my daughter will want to knit. I'll hold on to it, just in case.")

For some of you, it may be food. ("I hate bean soup, but I'm going to hold on to it just in case we run out of money and I'm not able to buy groceries.")

And finally, there's the one that every woman I know deals with: The Just in Case Wardrobe. Just in case I lose twenty pounds. Just in case I gain twenty pounds.

Fighting Just-in-Case Thinking

William Morris, the nineteenth-century English textile designer, reportedly said, "Have nothing in your house that you do not know to be useful or believe to be beautiful." Good advice to help us fight against just-in-case hoarding. I would state the same principle this way: Scale down to only what you need, and then add a bit of what you love.

But it's not easy to apply that principle consistently to help us fight just-in-case thinking. My friend Erin says her dad always takes an insurance policy on his insurance policies (you know, just in case the first insurance policy gets lost or something). It's funny, but the truth is that a lot of us live with insurance policies on top of insurance policies with our stuff. We always think we need more. Just in case.

But I'm learning it's not always so. In fact, sometimes less is the answer to our "just in case."

After my friend Cheri took a trip to Europe, she posted two pictures on Facebook: one of her and her husband, Daniel, and the tiny suitcases they took on their trip, and the other of the contents of her tiny suitcase that got her through hiking, fancy dinners, museum tours, and university visits.

Of course, being a "stuff expert," I was fascinated by the lack of, well, stuff. So I replied to her post with this: "I totally want to see a list of what you brought and then tell me how often you got to wash stuff out (and did you have access to washing machines, etc.). Fascinating!"

I won't reproduce here Cheri's packing list for her trip, but if you're interested in what little she managed to get by on, take a look at appendix 3. But let me just say, Cheri is my hero. She had to fight every just-in-case tendency in her body—and she won.

And her example challenges me to look at my packing, and my stuff in general, in a different way.

My tendency is to take everything I could ever conceivably need (and anything a complete stranger may need) with me, just in case. I have been known in the past (before my goal to live and travel clutter free) to travel with an extra coffee cup (just in case the motel has only small ones), some packets of coffee creamer (just in case the hotel has only powdered creamer and no Starbucks nearby), a portable printer (just in case I need to print a speech or boarding passes), and several extra pairs of shoes (just in case all my shoes develop holes in the soles and I have to resort to the old cardboard trick).

It's my natural leaning when it comes to packing.

And when I think of it, that's my natural leaning when it comes to my home as well. Something in me wants to hang on to everything, just in case.

At one point I had fifty plates just in case we had a big dinner party (Somehow, it doesn't occur to me that we only have room for about sixteen people in our house.)

I have hung on to DVDs just in case one of the kids wanted to borrow them.

I have hung on to an extra printer (that no longer worked well and made me want to fling it across a room anytime I did use it) just in case one of ours completely died.

Any of these on their own isn't a huge problem, but all combined? That's a garage full of just in case.

That leads me to a deeper issue. Why do I have to be prepared for every possibility? Why do I have to be the bottom line for everything?

I'm the one dragging around the giant messenger bag at Disneyland with the sunscreen, hand wipes, extra hat, and more for everyone in the family, just in case. Oh, and then they want me to hold their wallets, since I have a bag anyway. Why do I do it?

It's just fear.

Fear that I won't have enough. Fear that I will be stuck without something and not know what to do.

Fear Commands Us to Keep

If you give that wok away, you will need it again someday.

If you get rid of this book, you'll just want to read it again in six months.

If you get rid of this expensive jacket, your husband will think you're wasteful for giving it away.

So for the past several years, I've been intentionally fighting just-in-case thinking.

Right now, I'm at the cabin in the woods that my friend Sharon owns, and I did some radical packing in order to get here: I packed only one pair of shoes. I had the pair of black flip-flops on my feet, and then I packed only a pair of running shoes to go for long walks in the woods with my husband and dog.

And fear reared its ugly head. "What if your flip-flops break? What if two pairs of shoes for eight days isn't enough? What if you want more choices?"

But here we are on day four, and two pairs of shoes has been the exact right number. Not once have I thought, *Oh, I wish I would have brought...* In fact, 95 percent of the time when I bring something just in case, I end up leaving it in the suitcase, untouched.

Packing for a trip is a reflection of our packing in our lives. Am I constantly keeping things on my journey that are weighing me down?

As you process your clutter and those just-in-case thoughts rear their ugly heads, here are a couple of thoughts to fight back with:

"My security comes from God and not my possessions."

David reminds us where our security truly lies when he says in Psalm 56:3-4,

> When I am afraid, I put my trust in you.
> In God, whose word I praise—

in God I trust and am not afraid.
What can mere mortals do to me?

Yes—we need to be planners and wise with our resources, but that is not where our security comes from. I've never woken up in the middle of the night, panicked, and then soothed myself back to sleep with the comforting knowledge that I packed that extra pair of earrings.

"Most of these things I will never use again."

Of the one hundred things you keep just in case, how many will you ever use again? One? Two? Give it all away, and then buy the one or two things you will actually need again.

"I am up to the challenge of living with less in my everyday life."

Cheri's travel and packing adventure really made me think about the way I pack. No, she and I would never pack exactly the same, and there is no way I could pull off surviving for eighteen days out of a carry-on. But I could be more strategic in what I bring and challenge myself to use items in multiple ways.

The first time I challenged myself to pack only a carry-on was for an overnight trip—and it was a total success. Now? I'm up to five days. I'm writing this in the middle of that five-day trip that involves several meetings where I need to look my best—but I'm secure in the knowledge that no matter what, I'll live though the experience. And on this trip, which has been riddled with flight delays, I've been able to live lighter by not having to check luggage or wait around to pick it up.

What items around your home have you been hanging on to just in case? I don't want you to do anything with them at the moment (we'll get to that in the "Hands" section of the book), but I do want you to recognize them for what they are: false security blankets. And do you really want to be looking for your security in an extra waffle iron?

11

But So-and-So
Gave It to Me

Problem: We can't get rid of anything the people who love us have given us because it seems like it would be rejecting their love.

My friend Sarah raced upstairs to find her daughter Janessa in tears, sobbing about a ratty, dirt-smeared My Little Pony that her cousin Heidi was playing with.

"What's wrong?" Sarah asked, wondering what could've possibly set Janessa off, considering that she never had problems sharing with her cousin.

"I told Heidi she could have one toy in my room to keep, and she picked that My Little Pony."

"OK, that's OK," Sarah said, knowing it was a cheap toy that Janessa never played with.

"But my friend Annie gave it to me! And she'll know I don't love her if I give it away."

It's funny when we're talking about a five-year-old and a My Little Pony, but many of us operate under the exact same assumption: giving away a gift from someone we love is somehow equal to…not loving them.

If I give away grandmother's chair, even though it is unusable, my family members will think I didn't care about her.

If I give away this Hummel that my mom gave me, it will prove I'm an ungrateful daughter.

If I sell my grandmother's china that has been sitting in my garage for decades, I'm not honoring her legacy.

If I give the shirt my mom gave me to Goodwill, I'm showing that I didn't appreciate the gift, even though it went out of style back when I was in high school.

These are the guilty refrains you can hear all across America. And these are the familial legacies and gift-induced guilt-trips that are keeping us buried in stuff.

I told you that my friend Cheri and I spend a lot of time talking about clutter. One day I emailed her a deep philosophical question: What does it take for clutter to thrive in a home? She wrote back to me:

> Familial patterns + GUILT
>
> Daniel [Cheri's husband] simply can't imagine letting go of anything that anyone has ever given him. His family taught him that was the equivalent of throwing away their love. We had to dress our kids up in the clothes that relatives had given them and take photos, send the photos, make sure they were wearing those same clothes when they came to visit…regardless of how ugly or ill-fitting they were.

My mom is a quilter (and a talented one at that). When she gives me a quilt, I hang on to it, love it, and take great care of it. But when my mom gives me a shirt or a book, I love those things for a while and then pass them on to someone else. There is danger in giving the same value to every possession given to you by someone you love. When every possession is special, none of them are.

When it comes to gifts from relatives who are no longer living, I try to pare down to those things that bring back good memories and are indicative of the relationship I had with them.

My grandma Modesta (my father's mom) was a professional artist, so I've held on to a few paintings she did for me. My grandma Edna (my mom's mom) loved clothes and was proud of her German heritage. I kept her recipe box, a pair of silver art deco earrings, and a small silver box with her aunt's initials carved into it. Inside is a tiny note in German with warm wishes.

And for both my grandmothers, that is enough. Anything else would be extra. I get all I need from those items. Only two of those things serve a purpose (I use the recipe box and wear the earrings), but all the rest just bring me joy to look at. I don't have any of their things stuffed in a box, piled in a closet, or costing money in a storage locker.

But I know people who have their parent's entire household stored in their garage. They can't figure out what is OK to throw away, what is OK to give away, and what they should keep.

Here is another thing to think about: Are you perpetuating the clutter cycle for others by the way you give them things? Do things equal love in your mind?

You need to get rid of that kind of thinking. Things do not equal love.

"If my daughter-in-law loves me, she'd have the things I gave her displayed in her house." How messed up is that? We need to be intentional about the clutter burden we are imposing on others, whether it's the gifts we're giving or the legacy we are passing down.

My daughter is very clutter sensitive. She hates the burden of things she doesn't want or need. We've come to the conclusion that unless I've heard of something specific she wants or needs, it's just easier and less stressful for everyone if:

- I take her shopping.
- I give her a gift card.

She is *so* grateful when we do this. For some, it would take the fun out of it, but not for Kimberly. And while I like coming up with gifts for others, if it's truly about giving a gift to someone else, I don't have to do it on my terms.

It's one thing to change your thinking about getting rid of the things people give you, but here is some practical advice when it comes to dealing with it.

Take photos of the things others give you and save the photos for sentimentality.

Set a time limit.

Erin says, "When my mother-in-law would visit, she would always bring stuff. And lots of it. So I'd tell my kids, 'We're going to play with this stuff for a week, and then we're going to donate it to someone who wants it more.'"

Think of things as expendable, not permanent.

If someone gives you chocolate, you eat it. If someone gives you a vase of flowers, you enjoy them while they are fresh. So why not assume that if someone gives you a set of plates, you can use them and enjoy them and then pass them along to someone else.

Save a part of something for sentimentality.

Erin passed along this example and bit of advice:

> I have a mismatched set of teacups in my cabinet. My grandmother had eight sets of china, so each of her grand-children took two pieces from each set so we have a fun, mismatched set and can all enjoy all of them. Save a scrap of cloth to make a quilt or scrapbook. Save a plate or a mug from a china pattern.

I would rather display my grandmother's cookie jar on my hutch in the kitchen than have her entire set of stoneware packed in a box in the basement.

Have a swap.

My brother Brian had a huge set of BRIO trains when he was little. Fortunately, my mom saved them for my son, who was the world's authority on trains at four years of age. But when it was time for Brian's daughter to go through a train phase, the BRIOs went back to him. He's now saving them for when my kids have kids of their own.

I have a dollhouse that my dad built for me and that my grandmother, the artist, painted for me. My niece Elsa still uses and loves the dollhouse, but when that phase of her life is over, it will come back to me for my grandkids. We didn't save every toy—just a few that we knew were important. But we swap those back and forth depending on the ages of our kids.

Repurpose it.

If you love the brooch your Great-Aunt Vina gave you, but would never wear it in a lifetime and a half, find something else to do with it. Display it on a box, pin it to a decorative towel in your guest bathroom, attach it to a sachet in your closet where you can see it every morning when you get dressed.

If this is a problem you struggle with, here are some questions to ponder: *How am I advancing my relationship with this person by keeping this item? Is it blessing them? Is it blessing me?*

12

I'll Put It Here for Now

Problem: "I'll put it here for now" thinking has caused your home to not only be cluttered but also chaotic.

For most of us Clutter = Indecision.

Indecision of *where* things belong.

Indecision of *what* things belong.

I want you to do something for me right now. I know, you're probably all comfy on the couch, kicked back with your iced latte, enjoying a little peace and quiet and unclutter time. But you're going to have to get up. Do it just once. For me.

I want you to take a walk around your main living space (your kitchen, great room, living room, wherever it is that you spend most of your time) and count how many things are arbitrarily placed somewhere—not in a specific place where they belong but just somewhere because you put them there "for now."

I just did this same exercise (I'm not one to make my friends do something that I'm not willing to do myself), and I have to admit that I found ten "just there for now" items. There's the coffee cup my friend left at my house. It's sitting on the edge of the counter waiting for me to remember to take it to her. There's a CD I've been wanting to listen to and so I haven't put it away lest I forget. There's a dead plant that

I'm still meaning to try to rescue and a dead flower that I need to either press or throw away. And there's my go-to comfort cookbook that was pulled from the shelf in a moment of temporary insanity (I thought I was going to make a cheesecake. I was wrong.), only to be left on the coffee table for a week. And as bad as ten items sounds, five years ago that number would have been in the triple digits.

It's so easy to just put things somewhere "for now" and then leave them there day after day, week after week, month after month until our house becomes a cluttered mess.

This happens when we're at the store and can't decide if we need something or not, so we bring it home. Once it's home, we can't decide where it belongs, so we put it in a "temporary" place, and it adds to the cluttered landscape of our lives.

And it happens when we pull something out for a specific reason but then leave it out.

And it happens when we end up with something (a cup someone gives us, a book we borrowed), and we aren't really sure where to put it. So we put it anywhere.

And it happens when we are feeling overwhelmed and chaotic, and instead of putting something back where it's supposed to go, we leave it here "for now" and then wonder why our kitchen is always such a mess after we do something as simple as make a sandwich.

This is a dangerous place for us to be. Because when one or two things are out of place, it's easy to remedy. But when it happens day after day and week after week, suddenly we're left with a pile of things that have no home and a pile of stress that's difficult to overcome.

It happens so easily.

We don't know exactly where the mail goes, so we'll put it here for now.

Your son just joined Little League! Now there is his bag and his shoes and his hat. Where do they all go? We don't know, so we'll just put them there by the front door for now.

And then suddenly, we have piles of "I'll put it here for now" all over the kitchen counters, at the front door, and on our nightstands. Our office becomes an entire room dedicated to "I'll put it here for now."

It happens because we're too tired or busy or overwhelmed to *think*. If this is part of your clutter profile, here are three ways to attack it.

Assign a place for everything you intend to keep.

When thinking through where you want to put stuff, here are some questions that will help you decide.

How often will I use it?

In order for something to earn a place on my kitchen counter, under the island in the middle of the kitchen, or in the cabinets, it needs to be used almost every day. And I reevaluate this all the time.

On the kitchen counter we have:

- a coffee maker (mine)
- an espresso maker (my husband's)
- a toaster oven
- a standing mixer
- a blender
- a collection of oils, spices, and seasonings

Under our butcher-block island we have:
- pots and lids
- a slow cooker
- a juicer
- a rice cooker

In nearby cabinets we have:
- pans
- storage containers
- kitchen utensils
- plates, cups, and bowls
- silverware
- drinking glasses

For things that are not used as frequently, I have a red hutch in the eating nook that contains:

- serving platters
- serving bowls
- placemats and tablecloths
- a food processor
- extra silverware and plates for guests

Finally, for kitchen items that we use less than once a month, we have a white hutch in the garage. Yes, it's inconvenient to get to those items, but they keep us from having a cluttered kitchen and fight the "I'll put it here for now" problem.

What I have in remote storage:

- a fondue pot
- Thanksgiving supplies
- Christmas supplies
- seldom used baking pans (cheesecake pan, roasting pan)
- canning supplies
- a large stockpot

How pretty/ugly is it? Do I want it out in the open or behind cupboard doors?

I don't want a ton of knickknacks around my house, but I do want containers to hold everyday necessities. I had some big, beautiful canisters that were holding traditional canister items—flour, sugar, etc. Now I use them to house all my coffee supplies and keep those things in the open.

How hard to move is it? Do I need it out where I can always get to it?

This is part of the reason the standing mixer is on our counter. Some weeks I may use it only once, but I have a semi-irrational fear of dropping it on my foot and not being able to walk for a month. (Only semi-irrational since the thing weighs twenty-two pounds and I'm not the most graceful person in my household.)

Before buying something new, ask yourself, "What will I need to move, put away, or get rid of in order to make space for this?"

Cheri offers this example:

> Daniel wants to get a fresh pasta maker (an expected result of visiting Italy!). I'm refusing until he can tell me *exactly* where it will be stored. Otherwise, I *know* it will be set on one of our counters that's already crowded with his juicer, the toaster oven, microwave, fruit bowl, etc. So *no pasta maker* until there is a *plan for where to put it*! (Which has, thus far, stumped him so badly that I don't think we're gonna get one...whew!)

Train your brain to remember that whenever you say to yourself, "Just for now," that is the beginning of your next clutter pile.

Develop a hatred of things being out of place.

Last night was a rough night. I spoke at an event in Southern California yesterday morning, and had given myself plenty of time to get to my flight leaving out of San Diego.

Except I hadn't.

The traffic from my event to the airport, which should have taken an hour on a Saturday afternoon, took three and a half hours. So I booked another flight, had my ticket texted to my phone, dropped off the rental car, and made my way to the terminal.

When I went through security, my e-ticket was rejected at security. So I was sent back to the counter to get a printed ticket.

Did I mention that it was the weekend of Comic-Con in San Diego? Yep. Special times.

I got back into the security line, and then a buzzer went off. I was randomly selected to have an oddly personal search performed on me in the security area.

At that point, I just wanted to be done. I was so tired, so frustrated, and I just wanted to get on a plane and head to Denver where my friend Michele was waiting with barbecued hamburgers and a soft pillow to lay my head on. I jammed all my bags one into another and headed to the waiting area.

When I finally arrived in Denver, I grabbed a rental-car shuttle to take me to pick up my car. While on the shuttle, I got my reservation out and dug out my wallet to grab my license so I could speed away.

But my license? Nowhere to be found.

I dumped out my wallet and went through the entire contents of my computer bag. Nothing.

I was practically in tears. It was after midnight, six hours after I was supposed to arrive, and I still had another forty-five minutes ahead of me to get to Michele's place. I was on the ragged edge.

But I finally gathered myself together and repeated my steps. And that's when I remembered the last time I had my license: in line at the San Diego Airport. I found my handbag that I'd shoved into my clothes carry-on and sure enough, there was my license.

The reason I tell you this story is that even when we've trained our brain to hate the words "for now," we must be on guard against it when our resistance is low. We must develop an unease when things are out of place.

It takes only a moment to pull over to the side at the grocery store (or after a cavity search at the airport) to put things back where they belong.

And it's the same with our homes. If we can develop the feeling of being unsettled until we know that our stuff is back in its proper home, not only will it cut the clutter in our lives, it will save us the stress of having to constantly repeat the line, "I know I put it here somewhere…"

Here are a few ideas from Erin for how to avoid just putting stuff somewhere:

- I keep three baskets on my stairs—bottom step is Will, middle step is Kate, top step is Joey. Anything I find downstairs that belongs to my kids can be put in their basket for them to put away at the end of the day.

- Have a bin or basket for "returns or borrows." That's what takes up most of my clutter space—things that belong to other people and thus don't have a spot in our house.

- Keep a stack of small plastic bins in your house (I buy them in bulk) so when you have a new item that you don't know where to put, you have a storage spot. For example, my kids got Rainbow Loom rubber bands as a gift the other day, and they covered my floor five minutes later. We pulled out an empty bin, labeled it, put it in the toy bin, done. I also keep empty plastic bins on shelves in the kids' toy closet so there is never an excuse for "I didn't know where it goes."

What is causing you to put things down "for now"? Are you feeling too rushed in your everyday life? Is there never a chance to reset?

As you go through the process of clearing out your clutter, you will see that things become easier to put away when there is a home for them and that home is easier to access.

When you are tempted to put something down, ask yourself, "Will I really have more time to deal with this later? Will I know where to find this later when I'm looking for it?"

Be kind to your future self and put it away now. Next week you will thank me.

13

But I Spent So Much Money on It

I went to summer camp and fell in love. His name was Rich, and my fifteen-year-old brain convinced me he was the love of my life. But then our week of summer camp was over and all we had were letters back and forth. When school rolled around, I knew that things with Rich were not going well. We went from writing letters every day to every other week. When we called each other, we had nothing to say.

But when one of my friends suggested that I break up with him, I was aghast. "How could I? I have two whole months invested in this relationship."

As a grown woman, I now see the crazy wrapped up in that statement. Why would I hang on to a boyfriend who was not good for me, not worth the effort, and actually dragging me down just because I'd invested eight weeks in our "relationship"?

But how many bad relationships are you in that are not based on the value of time but of money? Here's a list of relationships I let go on too long because "I spent so much money on it":

- a leather jacket that I got on sale, and was still pretty

expensive, but it never quite fit right (I was going to lose a few—as in twenty—pounds.)

- a cell phone that needed to be rebooted a couple of times a day
- a pair of pumps that made my little toe bleed
- a dress that made my daughter itch and cry every time I put her in it
- a pot with a broken handle that I bought in Japan with a week's worth of wages (when I was twenty)

Some of those are small things that we keep around, hoping to find something redemptive to do with them. Other times, we keep our mistakes around in order to remind ourselves of what seems like a horrible, irreparable mistake.

Cheri's Story

My daughter was about to start high school, and I was fretting about her study habits: she didn't seem to have any. I kept telling her that her high school GPA would influence future college scholarship offers. (What I really meant, of course, was, "You're the child of two teachers. For Pete's sake, don't embarrass us with bad grades!") I offered her financial incentives (aka bribes). Nothing seemed to work.

One day, while worrying about Annemarie's future, I happened upon an infomercial for a series of amazing DVDs. They promised to teach my child spectacular study skills or my money back!

The price was out of our budget, about $100, but I was willing to sacrifice for the good of my child. I was in such a rush to order, I asked no questions and ignored all fine print.

When the DVDs arrived, Annemarie didn't just hate them. She openly mocked them. Nothing about the content or presentation style matched her learning style in any way, and boy did she let me know! I was so let down. Here, I'd thought I'd solved a major problem. But now the problem still wasn't solved, and I was out $100.

My disappointment was nothing compared to the shock I felt when our next Visa bill arrived. The $100 I'd paid turned out to be nothing more than a deposit. In my rush to order, I'd agreed to a monthly installment plan that would total almost $1000 by the end. When I called about returning the DVDs, I was told that the nonrefundable deposit, shipping, and restocking fees would total several hundred dollars.

So I kept those DVDs. I'd paid for them, and I was going to keep what I'd paid for, by golly. I kept them out in the open, where I could see them every time I walked by the family room. And those DVDs didn't just sit silently on a shelf. Oh no, they started mocking me:

"You thought you were actually going to solve a problem? That's a laugh! Around here, you *are* the problem, dumb blondie!"

"You were once good at math, but now you've paid $1000 when you thought you were paying $100. What on earth happened to you, ya lame loser?"

"You thought we were going to convince your daughter to study? What a cop-out! What kind of mother buys DVDs as a substitute for parenting?"

I kept those DVDs, and kept hearing their insults, for years. I told myself that I was saving them for Jonathon (who, it turned out, hated them as much as his sister did). But I was stuck in the belief that since I'd paid for them, I *had* to keep them. I also felt that I deserved to be *punished* for my impulse purchase: *I'm the one who made the mistake, so I'm the one who deserves to suffer.*

I finally donated those DVDs to a local school. Yes, it was

hard, in the moment. I kept telling myself, "After all the money I wasted on those, I should…"

But I couldn't finish the sentence any more. "I should…" what? Keep letting them gather dust? Keep mocking me day in and day out? Keep making me feel like an idiot?

The day I gave those DVDs away, I walked by the family room without flinching for the first time in years. Without being relentlessly reminded of a past mistake for which I'd long since repented and from which I'd learned my lesson.

How many of us have the DVDs in the room? (At least they're smaller than an elephant, right?)

But your "Memorial to Bad Financial Choices" probably looks a little different from Cheri's or mine. There are clothes in your closet, DVDs in your TV console, gadgets in your drawers, and knickknacks on your shelves that are reminding you how many bad choice you've made.

And for some reason, instead of letting the item go, we decide that we need to keep those items around for a number of twisted reasons.

I can fix it.

Several years ago, Roger was carrying a CorningWare stockpot that my mom gave us and tripped. That pot cracked right down the middle. Roger was so upset with himself—he knew how much I loved that pot. But it was an accident and there was nothing to be done about it.

But I couldn't bring myself to throw out those pieces. In my not-so-rational mind, I thought, *Well, there's nothing that will repair it now. But what if, someday, someone comes up with a way to repair it?* I know. Crazy thinking. But don't you have something hiding in your house that was really expensive, and you're waiting to repair it, someday?

I need to be reminded of how bad it was so I never do it again.

Like Cheri, we are so terrified of making the same mistake again, that we keep the item in plain sight so that we won't do it again. The ugly, uncomfortable chair that we keep for ten years because we spent so much on it in a moment of panic. The uncomfortable mattress that we never took back.

I have to keep it.

"Waste not, want not" has been passed down from thrifty grandma to thrifty granddaughter for decades, possibly centuries. We don't want to waste money, so we hang on to items out of some vague sense that it would be a sin to give them away.

I need to be punished.

No, we would never say this aloud, or maybe even think it. But some of us have things around that we know we spent way too much money on, and we feel like we need to suffer some kind of penance for it.

I should use it.

"I spent so much money on it, I should be using it every day."

I understand all those things our heads tell us. My head has told them to me repeatedly. But the problem is that our head is helping us hold on to clutter out of obligation, guilt, shame, and fear. And clutter only leads to more obligation, guilt, shame, and fear.

Peace is far more valuable than any amount of money you spent on an item.

14

Dealing with Other People's Clutter

My dad is a hoarder.

No, he's never been featured on a cable channel. No psychologist has ever come to his house and initiated an intervention.

Nope, I've been the one to do that. My mom has been fighting this battle their whole marriage. And it's been an uphill battle against a pile of old computer parts and *National Geographic*s from the sixties.

It's been that way ever since I can remember. My mom couldn't win the battle, but she did her best to contain it.

In the four-bedroom house we grew up in, my dad had two areas that were completely his: the office and the garage. The office was piled with stamps and computer parts. It was unusable to anyone but my dad.

When I say stamps, some of you may think we're talking about a couple of binders filled with stamps and paraphernalia. But as a hoarder, my dad had about forty boxes of binders, loose stamps, accessories, and postcards. Hoarders can't stop at a binder when a room can be filled.

The garage? It was worse. There were two paths in the garage: one to the mailbox and the other to a chair at a desk. Everywhere else? It was piled six feet high with electronic parts, Coke memorabilia, old maga-zines, and what appeared to the rest of the family to be junk.

When I was an adult, my parents decided to move for the first time in a couple of decades. It took six full-sized Dumpsters to clean out my dad's garage. There was almost nothing worth selling. It was all out-dated, unusable, undesirable junk.

I've seen my dad cry only twice: Once when his dad died, and again when we cleaned out his garage.

Both my mom and my brother tried to help him sort through the mess. Finally, it was down to me. It was the first time I honestly felt like my dad didn't like me—it was that hard for him to get rid of stuff.

Since people know that I write about organization, I often get asked if I watch the show *Hoarders*. I tell them I can't; it hits a little too close to home.

The Challenge of Clearing Other People's Clutter

Most of us have enough of a problem getting rid of our own stuff, but trying to deal with someone else's treasures can be near impossible.

And I have to admit, I had to go from being a bit of a bulldozer with "helping" my dad sort through this thing, to stopping to listen to why these things were important. All I saw was a bunch of junk. But my dad knew every story of how he acquired that switch or computer part. He knew who had given him what and how much he had paid for each thing. And all of it was important to him.

And I think that's why it feels so much easier to deal with other peo-ple's things than our own. With other people's junk, there is no history for us. But with our own junk, we know the emotional and financial cost of each item. That's why it's so hard for us to give anything away.

As logical as it is to give away someone else's things, we have to tread lightly. And as much as it annoys us, people need to have a say in how their stuff is dealt with. When you're in a mindset to get rid of stuff, it's easy to look at your husband's, child's, or coworker's things and come to the all-too-reasonable conclusion, "Well, they haven't used it in five or ten or twenty years, so of course it's OK to get rid of it."

But the law of throwing someone else's stuff out is that as soon as you do, they will come looking for that thing that they haven't looked at in twenty years.

Here is Cheri's experience with clearing other people's clutter, specifically her husband's stuff:

> While Daniel was gone for a weeklong trip, I decided to "gut the garage." Our last move was four years ago, and we still had close to a hundred boxes, many labeled "stuff" and still taped shut. I knew what was in some of them, but most I did not.

> Because I'd done so much decluttering of my own, I was on a ruthless, take-no-prisoners rampage to rid the garage of anything we didn't need. Here, I made two mistakes: first, I was aware only of my own mindset, not Daniel's. And second, I defined "anything we didn't need" as "anything I don't use."

> I told myself that I was doing all this work while Daniel was gone "to surprise him." But that was only part of the truth. I was also doing it so that he couldn't see what I was giving away. That was my third mistake: being sneaky, even deceptive. I'd convinced myself that what he didn't know couldn't hurt him. But this was not a decision for me to make for him.

> By the final day, I was so sick and tired of stuff that I really didn't care anymore. If it took up space, I was ready to give it away. As a result, I ended up taking a collapsible Black & Decker tool bench to Goodwill, unaware that (a) it had been a gift from my father to Daniel, and (b) Daniel used it frequently.

> A few weeks later, while I was traveling, Daniel needed to saw some boards for a project in his classroom. When he couldn't find the work bench or his circular saw, he texted me in frustration. He felt disrespected by my invasion of his property. While this was never my intention, I must admit that I had not put any effort into prevention.

Here are some ways to avoid my mistakes:

1. Recognize the danger of having a new mindset.

In Celebrate Recovery circles, it's known that there's nobody more annoying than someone new to recovery. Their eyes have been opened, and now they expect everyone else to magically "get it" too.

It's easy to forget that it took them years, perhaps even decades, to change their mind. It's not fair—or respectful—to expect others to change overnight.

2. Plan to have numerous small conversations about "the stuff."

Your goal isn't to persuade the other person to adopt your paradigm. Your goal is to understand their position so you know where the lines are. Some questions you might discuss include:

- What space is mine? Yours?
- Which items are mine? Yours?
- What would you like me to do with your stuff when it outgrows its allotted space? (Move it into your room? Rent a storage facility and move it there?)

3. Focus your time and energy on your stuff.

It's all too easy to hyper-focus on the speck in someone else's eye while ignoring the plank in our own (Matthew 7:3-5). If I'm honest, part of my reason for meddling with my husband's stuff was that it felt like a nice distraction from dealing with the rest of my own stuff.

But what I know from many past experiences, when I simply lead by example, others often (but not always) follow (although rarely on my time schedule!). It's far more productive for me to mind my own stuff than to stick my nose into someone else's stuff.

4. Ask about one thing at a time.

Daniel's biggest complaint was that I hadn't asked him about any of the items I gave away. At the time, I felt justified; after all, there was so much stuff and so little time. Now, with some distance, I realize that I violated a basic human right and need: we all want to have a say in what happens to us and our belongings.

I really didn't need to be in such a hurry. It's not like we were moving or needing to have a garage sale to raise money. I'd picked an arbitrary deadline that created urgency. This urgency allowed me to justify my methods, but it was false urgency.

Make a list of everything that you'd like to get rid of. Start asking, one item at a time, and record the answers you receive. Look for patterns. Prayerfully reflect on alternative solutions when you are told no.

5. Accept and, when possible, improve what you cannot remove.

Our garage still has several dozen boxes of Daniel's stuff. But instead of cardboard boxes with *stuff* written across the side, it's all stored in large clear bins. Yes, they cost some money. But now Daniel can actually see what is in them. When he needs something, he can tell which bin to pull out. Being able to see the contents removes some of the fear of the unknown.

Tips to Help Guide Your Conversation

What I've learned from Cheri's experience and my own is that this is dangerous territory. I've also learned a few tips to help the conversation along the way.

Agree on space, time, and financial limits.

My mom wanted a nice, comfortable house. My dad wanted his stuff. So they came to an agreement: He got the garage and his office to do with whatever he wanted. I don't know that they ever spoke that agreement aloud, but that's how it came down.

If you have someone in your life who is entrenched in their stuff, you may not be able to "fix" them, but you may be able to limit the impact it has on the rest of your family.

Agree on space limits. Have a conversation about the amount of space that can be dedicated to their stuff. You are not controlling which of their things they keep, only agreeing to the amount of space it's allotted. Maybe each of you has six Rubbermaid tubs in the craft room, or each has one unit of shelving in the garage. One person's office could be completely theirs. You have no say in what is in the room, but if their stuff starts to migrate into the common areas of the house, you can remind them that you've agreed to keep certain areas off limits.

Agree on time limits. If you have *National Geographic*s from the seventies that you're hoping will be worth something someday, let me tell you, they won't. My son works at a very busy used bookstore in a very hip part of Northern California. They sell each copy of *NG,* regardless of date or subject matter, for fifty cents. Yes, you may have individual copies you could sell on eBay for a bit more, but is it worth taking up a car's worth of space in your garage?

If they are worth something, then figure it out together. Do your research. But when you find out that 99 percent of them are virtually worthless, it's time to dispose of them. Six months seems like a reasonable amount of time to figure out how to get as much value out of them as you can.

Some organizational experts suggest that you put a date on boxes of stuff that you've gone through. If you haven't gone into a box in six months or a year, donate that box without opening it.

This won't work with someone who has a tendency to hoard. They won't be willing to give away a box that they can't go through again. How about in six months, you agree that you will each get rid of two boxes of stuff?

Agree on financial limits. In order to lessen the resentment in their relationship, my parents hit on a solution that worked for them. My dad, the collector, and my mom, the fabric buyer, each had an amount of money they could spend each month that didn't need to be discussed or agreed on nor did they need to feel guilty about it. Anything beyond that amount needed to be agreed on by both of them. It may not lessen the space that is taken up, but it will lessen the tension when it comes to stuff.

Be a great example.

Make sure you are growing in your dealings with your own stuff. Make the hard decisions and share it with your family. "Yes, I know that those books may have some value, but space is more valuable to me than any amount of money I could get for them."

Let your kids know that getting rid of stuff is a part of your life process. It has to happen regularly, not just when you can't move around in your home anymore.

Work on small spaces.

Don't overwhelm the collector. Start with a drawer, a box, a bag, or a shelf. If you say, "We are going to clean out this room!" that is completely overwhelming. "Small and well" beats "big and yelling at each other" every time.

My final tip: *pray*. I know that sounds a little extreme. It's just clutter, right? But our clutter is a part of us. One person's clutter is another person's 1994 Beanie Baby. Pray, and be respectful, loving, and firm.

It is possible to live in a space that you love, even with someone else's stuff.

15

I Want to Be the Kind
of Person Who...

Problem: We are trying to buy the kind of life we want, instead of living the kind of life we want.

My friend Erin told me that in college, she saved up several months' paychecks from her student work-study job to buy a pair of leather pants. Yes, leather pants. The staple of every college student's wardrobe.

Erin said that after watching the movie *Grease*, the picture of Sandy and her gorgeous hair just wouldn't get out of her head. And she just knew that if she had a pair of leather pants, she would be as hip and cool and smart as Sandy.

So she bought those leather pants.

She loved them for a few weeks—while they were new—but she quickly found out what most of us already know: leather pants aren't exactly a comfy option for an 8:00 a.m. class. And they certainly aren't a good wardrobe choice for dinner with grandparents. And if you've ever worn leather pants (oh, wait, you haven't?), you would know that they are hot and sticky and ridiculously uncomfortable.

And so Erin's leather pants hung in her closet. And months turned into years. Years into decades. And Erin never turned into Sandy. But she does still have a pair of black leather pants hanging in her closet as a reminder that the things you buy do not make you who you want to be. As nice as that would be.

In the book industry, there is a style of book called Chick Lit. Think *Bridget Jones's Diary* and *The Devil Wears Prada*.

I like Chick Lit. But my husband says that my favorite type of book is actually Chicken Lit. Any book that has to do with simple living, farm living, gardening, raising livestock, or setting up a chicken coop in your backyard? That's what I want to spend my afternoon reading.

I picture myself picking fresh blackberries (you know, so I can make homemade jam with the raw sugar I made yesterday from sugar beets) while checking on the animals and…obviously I have a problem when I think I can become a homesteader in my townhouse out in the burbs.

But I still love these books. And as a result of reading them, I've taken on some simple living activities even from my suburban spread. I bake my own bread, I make my own laundry soap, and I hang our laundry to dry. We get 90 percent of our produce from a CSA (Community Supported Agriculture), I cook most of our meals from scratch, and we have a garden on our tiny patio that produces the best tomatoes you (or the neighborhood squirrels) have ever eaten. All of these things are activities that add to our home and that I enjoy.

But other activities have proven to me that I may not be cut out for life on the homestead.

- My attempts at homemade cheese, unlike my bread, have fallen flat.

- I can't sew my own clothes, even after years of home ec and sewing lessons.

- I want to make thoughtful homemade gifts for people, but on more than one occasion, I have run to the mall on December 23, trying to buy my way out of a Christmas gift meltdown.

My problem is I want to be the kind of person who does everything from scratch, and I've done the easy work of anyone who ever thinks to themselves, *I want to be the kind of person who...* What's the easy part? I bought all the stuff. And I mean *all* of it.

- I have all the tools and weird ingredients for DIY cheese.
- I kept until I was in my forties the sewing kit my mom made me in junior high.
- Through three moves, I kept all the supplies from failed attempts at Christmas gifts.

Buying to Become

When we buy to become, we are taking shortcuts to the results we want to have in our life.

And because of this, I've reached the conclusion (I know, I can be a bit slow) that when my only action is buying things and never doing (buying the cheese-making book but never making cheese, buying the canning jars but never canning,), those things become the clutter that crowds out the rest of my life.

Like Erin and the leather pants, and me and my faux homesteading supply closet, you might be trying to buy your way into a life that you have no business living.

Maybe you want to be the kind of mom who makes Pinterest-worthy snacks for your child's playgroup. Or the kind of friend who sends thoughtful, homemade cards. You want to be the kind of wife who bakes a cheesecake for your husband's birthday or the kind of woman your friends can always run to when they need a certain home-schooling resource.

I get it. We've all held on to things, we've all gone out and bought things, that we didn't use but wanted to, because we wanted to be the kind of person who...

Cheri, for example, had a dream for who she wanted to be:

Bump! Bang! Bash!

I should have checked immediately...walked out my classroom door to see about the commotion. But right as

I decided to halt instruction (for what felt like the hundredth time that hour), the hallway noises fell silent.

Later, I noticed.

Yeah, I should have checked immediately. Evidently a couple of nameless boys were roughhousing when they slammed into the display case.

The one I paid for. With my own money.

Replacing the Plexiglas would cost the same as replacing the entire display case. So I'm faced with

- leaving it (ugly)
- replacing it (costly)
- removing it (time-consuming)

I'm not just upset with the boys who broke something for which I'd paid good money. I'm upset with myself for buying those cases in the first place.

You see, this is one of four display cases that I ordered and had mounted on the wall outside my classroom. My vision was that I would become the kind of teacher who displays student work. Their writing. Their art. Their photography.

But that was several years ago, and all that's in this one display case is a poster promoting a writing contest to my seniors. The other three display cases are empty.

Why? Oh, we could be here all day exploring the answer to *that* simple question. For starters, I'm nonvisual, overcommitted, and global-abstract (rather than concrete-specific).

But the truth is that this was a purchase fueled by broken thinking.

Yes, I'm frustrated that the boys broke the display case. But not just because of the money. Mostly, it's because they made more obvious something that was broken from the

start: the idea that if I buy ___, I'll become someone who
___.

For me, it was the idea that if I bought the display cases, I'd
become someone who displays student work.

You probably haven't bought a display case (or four) recently. But
perhaps you've bought...

- a size-whatever dress in hopes you'll become someone who
  has a size-whatever body
- a gourmet cookbook so you'll become someone who cooks
  amazing gourmet meals
- a stenciling/scrapbooking/stamping/whatever-craft-is-hot-
  for-women-to-do-these-days kit, believing that this time
  you'll become someone who stencils/scrapbooks/stamps/
  crafts

Buying something to become someone who... is a temptation year-
round. But for me, it peaks in December. Everywhere I look, I see
women who so-and-so better than I do. And it's so easy to believe that
if I buy such-and-such, then I will become someone who so-and-soes
too!

This is a jarring reminder that buying something to become someone wastes the resources God's entrusted to me. And ultimately, buying to become wastes the someone God has already paid for me to be.
Here's how the apostle Paul expresses it: "You do not belong to yourself, for God bought you with a high price" (1 Corinthians 6:19-20 NLT).

- What items are you most likely to "buy to become"?
- What does it mean to you, in the midst of your daily life,
  that "God bought you with a high price"?

Resisting the Temptation

So how do we stop the habit of buying to become? Here are a couple of ideas to align our hearts and our stuff.

Focus on one new passion at a time.

No, I can't get the chickens I want. But I can have a garden in our backyard, and I can bake bread. And I haven't given up on mastering the art of cheese making. But as I adopt these new activities into my life, I'm adding only one new thing at a time. Right now it's cheese making. (I will conquer the mozzarella!) Once I've decided whether I am a cheese artisan, only then will I move on to my next endeavor: canning. And I will not buy any canning supplies until such a time as I am ready to can.

Take baby steps.

When I bought my cheese-making supplies, I had a few options, from the "I'd like to try to make a ball of mozzarella" kit to the "I plan on opening up a cheese shop in my backyard and need a three year's supply of ingredients." Before my clutter-free days, I would have gone all in. My thinking would have been, *I'm sure I'm going to love this! After all, I love cooking, so I'll just get everything so I don't have to wait to make my next batch of cheese.* Now I see the wisdom of taking things a (baby) step at a time.

Bless someone else with your failed experiments.

So you figured out that watercolors aren't your retirement plan. Don't hang on to those brushes and canvases for too long. Jump on Facebook and put out an all call to see who else has some Bob Ross fantasies floating around.

Buying to become often comes from that heart feeling of shame—I am not good enough as I am. Before you buy again, ask yourself these questions:

- Does this item fit with my current life or a life that I hope to have when I lose twenty pounds or have more time or start cooking from scratch?

- Do I have someone else in mind that I'm trying to impress with this purchase?

- How do I think this will change my life if I purchase it?

16

It Might Be Worth Something Someday

Problem: We are cluttering up our lives by investing in things that have no current value.

Really, people. Have Beanie Babies taught us nothing?

Back when Beanie Babies were at the height of their popularity, I was a sales rep for a number of different gift lines, including a plush animal company. Even though the line I was representing was a knock-off of the real Beanie Babies, people were losing their minds collecting our little animals.

Ty Inc. did a great job of creating a scarcity mentality when it came to those bags of beans. I remember setting up a display in a Hallmark store and there being a line of over a hundred people waiting to buy a new "limited edition" bear. When the gate was finally pulled up and the crowd pressed in, I had to leap out of the way to not be crushed by grown men who needed that cute yellow bear.

An article in the *LA Times* describes how Ty Inc. founder Ty Williams kept the Beanie Babies value artificially inflated:

> First, he adopted the distribution model for higher-end plush toys, selling Beanie Babies through specialty gift and

toy shops rather than through Wal-Mart, Toys R Us or other giant chain stores. That way, you couldn't find the entire line in one place, and buyers would seldom encounter piles of unsold Beanies—enhancing their status as collectibles, not mere commodities.

Not only did Warner keep introducing new Beanie characters, but he sometimes made changes in a line when he wasn't satisfied with the style or color. Thus, an orange Digger the Crab gave way to a richer red Digger after a year. Suddenly, collectors swooped on the scarcer original version, eventually bidding it up to $600 or more on the resale market—perhaps five times what a red Digger might bring.

Warner discovered he could create the same effect by abruptly ceasing production of a character. Without warning, he would announce such "retirements" on the Ty Inc. website, sending collectors scrambling all over again (Thomas S. Mulligan, "Another '90s Bad Dream," *Los Angeles Times*, August 26, 2004).

It's easy to scoff at people who spent hundreds, maybe thousands, of dollars on tiny toys thinking there was some sort of value to them. But think about the things sitting in your garage that you've vaguely thought, *Well, I should hold on to it. It might be worth something someday.*

I get it. With shows like *Antiques Roadshow* and *Pawn Stars,* we've all had dreams of finding a hunk of junk in our garage, showing it to an expert, and discovering that we've just paid for our retirement in a little cabin in the woods because of Grandma Trudy's locket that we found in a box of junk.

But I don't think that's what keeps us from getting rid of stuff. I think it's fear.

I think the real fear is that we will give away something of value. The possibility of regret keeps us from culling through the boxes in our attic. Oh sure, we may be brave enough to throw out an old TV or a broken chair, but what about the things that may have value.

And I'm not just talking about financial value.

In this brief exchange from the television show *The Big Bang Theory*, Sheldon and Leonard reflect this mindset of misplaced value:

> *Sheldon*: "So pay attention. Years from now, my biographer might ask you about this event."
>
> *Leonard*: "Oh, I have so many things to tell your biographer."

Sheldon, a genius scientist, believes that everything that has ever happened to him, or will happen to him, should be recorded for his future biographer to report on. He saves every paper he works on because he is just convinced that it's going to be important to someone, someday.

I've felt that way about my kids' schoolwork and art projects. I held on to every math test, every spelling test, every scrap of paper. I guess I was saving it because, hey, maybe they will want to look at it all someday.

Here is the truth: They will *not* want to look at all of it someday. They will want to look at some of it, maybe, someday.

(And if your kids are adults, what are you doing storing their stuff anyway? Stop that!)

Cull the best and get rid of the rest. And if you can't decide what is the best for someone else, have them help you. Your child will know that the fourth-grade math quiz is not important to keep, but the note that her best friend sent her saying that Mark has a crush on her? That might well be a keeper.

Here's the problem: I don't want to admit that much of what I'm surrounding myself with and spending my time maintaining is not of value. So it's easier just to ignore it and let the piles accumulate.

What's a Collector to Do?

So what do you do if your inner voice is letting you know that something might be valuable someday?

Get it checked out.

If you have an idea that something is "worth something," find a knowledgeable friend or professional and get it checked out. When you find out that the football signed by Abe Lincoln just might not be authentic, you can get rid of it and not feel guilty.

Limit the size of your treasure box.

Back in the day, our grandmothers had hope chests where they kept all their valuables: tea sets, love letters, wedding veils, and Aunt Vina's jewelry. They knew where their valuables were and they were well cared for.

Put your valuables where you can see them.

If your artifacts are of great sentimental value, put them where you can see and enjoy them. Stuffed in a box in the basement means they are not valuable to anyone.

Erin says, "My in-laws bought a thousand kinds of baseball cards in hopes they could sell them for retirement. You know how that goes. If you're using *things* as a retirement policy, then you are investing in the wrong thing."

If your collections are out of control, find out the truth about what you're collecting. Don't hang on to things out of a vague sense of "someday." If you love it, keep it and enjoy it. If not, get rid of it and make room for the most important things in your life.

17

But I Have So Much Invested in It

There is a time for everything,
and a season for every activity under the heavens…
a time to plant and a time to uproot…
a time to search and a time to give up,
a time to keep and a time to throw away,
a time to tear and a time to mend…
(Ecclesiastes 3:1-2,6-7)

King Solomon had a lot to say in the book of Ecclesiastes about the health of having things come to an end (and here you thought these words of wisdom were from Pete Seeger's song "Turn! Turn! Turn!" made famous by the Byrds).

There are others who get this better than I do. Farmers, for instance, understand there is a time for everything, and their lives revolve around the natural seasons of planting, tending their crops, harvesting, and letting their land lie fallow.

For the rest of us, we have problems with ending things. Somehow, in our society, we have come to the conclusions that relationships, projects, and other commitments should go on forever. That to stop is a sign of failure.

Four years.

That's how long we paid for the gym membership that he never used.

During my first marriage, my husband insisted that he needed that gym membership. Whenever I asked about canceling it, the question always came back, "Don't you want me to be healthy?" And my thought was, *Yes, I want you to be healthy. That's why I want you to go to the gym. But you don't. So let's cancel it.*

But that would have been admitting defeat. To cancel the membership would have been the equivalent of saying, "I'm too lazy to go."

And while it's easy for me to judge my ex-husband's gym membership, we all have our own "gym memberships":

- the meal planning website we pay $9.95 a month for and never use
- the guitar on the top shelf of the closet that was last played in youth group—fifteen (or more) years ago
- the book you were dying to read and that has sat on your shelf for the past five years
- the recording equipment you bought to cut your first album
- the supplies you bought to make your mosaic table
- the ski pants

Coming to Terms with Endings

Why is it so hard to get rid of these types of things? Because it means admitting that there is an ending.

And endings? They terrify us.

In our world, endings (whether they be projects, jobs, or relationships) equal failures. We hang on to art supplies we've never used, gifts from people we never liked (whether the person or the gift), and textbooks from classes we never completed.

"I really didn't know that things are supposed to end," Cheri told me. "At forty-seven, I really did not know. To me, end equals failure and failure equals worst thing in the world, to be avoided at all cost. So all my life, I've been trying to keep things going—*all the things* going. When you're a teenager in a dysfunctional family, that's hard enough. But by midlife, there are *too many things* and you cannot keep them all going."

And that's the problem: there is just too much—too many opportunities, too many projects, too many plans. And unless we let some of them go, we will never have the room for the life we are supposed to live.

When I'm making these kinds of decisions, I refer to the highlighted portions of the book *Necessary Endings: The Employees, Businesses, and Relationships that All of Us Have to Give Up in Order to Move Forward* by Henry Cloud. Now when Dr. Cloud was writing this book, I'm pretty sure that clutter was not at the forefront of his mind. The entire book is worth reading, but when I'm trying to get rid of the stuff in my life, three quotes from his book stand out to me:

> "*Without the ability to end things, people stay stuck, never becoming who they are meant to be, never accomplishing all that their talents and abilities should afford them.*"

Clutter makes us stuck. We can't start a new project because the reminders of all the old, unfinished projects tell us the lie, "Don't start something else. You never finish anything!" If you're anything like me, sometimes you start a project (knitting, say) and then realize that it's not relaxing for you, you have no natural ability, and everything you make looks like the potholder you made for your mom in fourth grade. For years you thought she proudly hung it on the wall because of its beauty, but at thirty, you realized it was because she didn't want to sustain third-degree burns on her hands.

And stuck? Is a horrible place to live.

I think one of the reasons for the high correlation between clutter and depression is the fact that people slowly stop doing the things that bring them joy (crafting, connecting with other people, creating, cooking) because there is so much stuff around them that keeps them stuck.

We need to end some of our relationships. Yes, some of those relationships are with people, but some of those relationships that we need to end are with stuff.

When we hang on to our daughter's baby clothes, waiting for her to have a daughter, even though she said she doesn't know if she'll have kids, we get stuck in the decisions of someone else's life.

When we won't pull out our sewing supplies because we feel so guilty about the scrapbooking supplies sitting on our craft table, we're stuck.

When we won't have a friend over because there is so much clutter, we're stuck.

When we give up on fixing up our home because there are so many projects we started and never finished, we're stuck.

When we won't cook dinner because it's hard to operate in a cluttered kitchen, we're stuck.

And we're stuck because we're not willing to end things. But we must realize that endings are a natural and healthy part of life.

> *"All of your precious resources—time, energy, talent, passion, money—should only go to the buds of your life or your business that are the best, are fixable, and are indispensable."*

Are the best.
Are fixable.
Are indispensable.

That is where my time, energy, talent, passion, and money should be going. Not the belt that makes me look like a Vienna sausage that's been cut in half. Not the broken mixer that no longer has parts available, but I hang on to anyway since it cost so much money. Not the six pairs of running shoes that I never wear.

Best.
Fixable.

Indispensable.

These are the things I need to surround myself with. These are worth my time and energy, my attention and cabinet space.

> *"One of the most important types of decision making is decid-ing what you are not going to do, what you need to eliminate in order to make room for strategic investments."*

We have to make some "end of life" decisions. At what point do we say, "This part of my life is over, not because I've failed, but because I have to make room for the things in my life that are growing and working"?

We have only a finite amount of space.

We have only a finite amount of time.

We have only a finite amount of energy.

We have only a finite amount of money.

We can't keep collecting things, lying to ourselves about our capac-ity to care for them.

We can't maintain all the relationships that look interesting and fun.

At some point, we need to end some things so we can hold on to the things that are most important to us. And when we define the things that are truly important to us, we can start recognizing the things that are not important to us and eliminate those things from our life.

I am not a foodie. I would have to know way more about olive oils and reductions to be labeled as such. But my one hobby is cooking, with a little food gardening thrown in. (My family would say reading as well, but that's also part of my work, so I always count that as job time.)

I've tried to get into other hobbies, but they just don't take. Give me a cookbook and something from the farmers' market, and I'm as happy as a pig in the Dumpster of a Krispy Kreme.

So any other "hobby" items I may come across in my life? I need to ditch them. They are taking up space and energy that I'd rather give to cooking.

What if someone said to you, "You have four guilt-free hours to yourself." What would you do with them?

For me, it would be to try a new recipe or go browsing in our local culinary tools store, read a cookbook or get on the phone with my friend Michele and talk recipes for an hour. (You need to have friends who are as weird about your hobbies as you are. The last time I visited Michele, I brought her a new protein powder and eight Madagascar vanilla beans. She received these treasures as if I were bringing her a bouquet of flowers and a diamond bracelet.)

But what if your reaction to the four guilt-free hours was, "I can't do anything because I'd need all that time just to clear a space in my office. I guess I'll watch TV"? If that's your reaction, that's a clear indication you need to make room for the things that are truly important to you.

Making Room for What Is Truly Important

Here are a few rules to live by when it comes to endings.

It's OK to realize you've outgrown something.

For years, my daughter and I loved the show *Gilmore Girls*. We watched it a lot. My kids bought me seasons of the show on DVD and I loved them.

But as I got a bit older, I realized that I wasn't enjoying them as much. While there were characters that I would adore forever (Sookie!), I started to see how self-centered the main character was. While it's still a great show, I can't see myself watching it again and so I passed the DVDs on.

Similarly, there may be things in your life that you have outgrown, even if at one time that activity was really important to you. Cheri says that her husband, Daniel, was an avid golfer, until every time he would hit the links, his swing would destroy more than the ball—it would also wreck his back. There may be a time for you to give away your field hockey stick, your skis, even your badminton rackets. Let someone else use and love them and keep the pictures of when you looked like a celebrity on the slopes.

Or maybe you have all the supplies to wash your car—but you haven't washed your car in years. You pay the extra ten dollars to run it through the wash when you gas up. You couldn't do that ten years ago—money was too tight. But now that things are a little easier, you would rather pay to go through the carwash than do it yourself.

And that's OK. Get rid of your car wash stuff. (Unless you have teens who will soon be driving. Then teach them to save the ten bucks. Car washes are for people who have disposable income.)

It's OK to admit it's not important to you.

I had someone give me a book on understanding this very deep theological aspect of the great tribulation. To some people, that's really important. I'm not smart enough to worry about it. I know where I'm going when I die. That's about all I can handle. It's not important to me (and one of the beautiful things about getting older is figuring out what isn't important to you), so I can give the book away.

You can spend a lot of money, time, and energy on something, and it can still be OK to admit that it's over.

Last week was a huge blogger conference held in my hometown of San Jose, California. Since I'm a blogger and it was in my hood, I had made the decision to go about six months ago.

What I couldn't have known at the time I made the reservation was all the ways my life was going to come crashing down around my head: the death of a family member, overwhelming work deadlines, my father's illness, and some medical challenges for myself. But my work deadlines were the day before the conference, so I thought, *Great, I'll get those over with and go to the conference.*

But when my deadlines were done, I didn't want to go to the conference. I wanted to stay home with my husband, and our dog, and not worry about what was going on in the real world. Plus a couple of my friends had attended the preview day and said, "You aren't missing anything. It's not that great this year."

The voices in my head were having none of that. They kept reminding me, "You *paid* for that ticket. You are on such a tight budget. You can't let that money go to waste."

Now that ticket was not physical clutter, but it had the same effect. It told me I couldn't do what I wanted because of the shame of wasted money, time, space, or energy.

After thinking about it for a little while, I came to a new conclusion: that ticket had bought me a weekend off.

If I hadn't paid for that ticket, I would have said yes to something else. There was an event I was asked to speak at and a party I was invited to. If I hadn't bought that ticket, I would have filled up my weekend with other commitments.

The price of that ticket bought me a weekend at home with my husband and my dog. And that is exactly what I needed at that moment. A little bit of peace.

How many times do we hold on to clutter because of what we've spent on it: in money, in time, in energy. We've committed a portion of our life to it, and we are reluctant to give it up because we've made such an investment. But those are sunk costs. You are never going to get that money or time back. What you need to consider is not how much it cost you before, but what it's worth to you today, right now.

It's OK to realize that something has become clutter.

When you start to call unfinished projects what they are—clutter— it gives you a whole new perspective on projects you're going to start.

In my twenties, if something sounded interesting, I would jump into it. Buying an audiotape course to learn how to speak Japanese? Sure, why not. All the supplies to make my own handcrafted paper? Let's go for it.

But when I start processing the leftovers of those long forgotten projects, I can't help but learn a little bit about myself:

- I have no natural aptitude for languages. Three years of Spanish tutors and a year living in Japan and still not being able to ask for directions to the noodle house attest to that.
- I am not, and never will be, a crafter.

Learning these two little truths about myself, now that I'm older and a little wiser, has kept me from getting sucked in to buying and starting projects. I'm finally learning from my mistakes.

Remember, clutter is anything you don't currently use or love, or anything you wouldn't pay for again. We can keep clutter from entering into our home by knowing ourselves and the likelihood of whether we will use an item or see a project through to completion.

As you process your clutter, determine the things that need to end in your life and get rid of them. Not because you failed, but because you are intentionally making room for the things that are truly important to you.

18

What If I Don't Have Enough?

When I was in junior high, I dreamed of the perfect high school experience. I would have a cute boyfriend who wore an acid-washed jean jacket and parachute pants. I would be a cross between the girls on *The Cosby Show* and Madonna—in other words, my bustier would be covered in an IZOD cardigan. We would listen to Bruce Springsteen and Culture Club on my boom box. I would drive around town in my Volkswagen Rabbit (with the top down, of course) and go shopping at the mall with my friends for jelly bracelets and neon leggings.

Dare to dream, baby.

But fantasy did not meet reality. My dad lost his job my freshman year of high school, and it was up to my mom to make ends meet. She performed miracles, but sadly, there was little money left over for the extra pairs of leg warmers my eighties teen heart so desired.

So I got a job to be able to afford all that I wanted. I thought with working after school I would be able to have the wardrobe and lifestyle of my dreams.

But when I compared my paycheck (with all its deductions) with the prices of the Ralph Lauren jeans I wanted at the department store,

I realized my dreams of walking off the pages of *Seventeen* magazine were not going to come true.

So instead of shopping at nice stores and getting the clothes I really wanted, I would go to the cheap stores—you know, the ones where clothes are piled on sales tables with "3 for $20!" signs on them, and the first time you wash your new purchase it turns into a wrinkled heap—so I could have a ton of clothes. The problem was, I almost never wanted to wear any of them a second time.

I had a stuffed closet but nothing to wear. Every time I looked in there, all I saw were mistakes and impulse purchases, and all I felt was regret that I didn't have the wardrobe of my dream.

But I told myself a lie when it comes to clothes: the more choices I have the happier I will be.

And here was the other problem: because I never felt like I had enough, I couldn't get rid of anything. My twisted thinking made me hang on to absolutely everything—no matter how out of style, ill-fitting, or downright ugly it was—because I was terrified of not having something that I might want, someday. Or what if I was looking through a magazine and saw that shirt I bought and the exact right way to accessorize it, but I'd just given it away.

It wasn't that I just feared not having enough—I feared the regret of giving something away. So instead of having a few things I loved, I settled for dozens of things that I didn't, but they made me feel safe.

And that is just wrong.

The Lies We Tell Ourselves About...

And sadly, even after I became an adult, this didn't apply just to clothes. It happened in other areas of my life.

Food

When I would go on trips, I would stuff enough snacks in my bag so that if I was stuck on a plane for ten hours, I wouldn't go hungry. (I've never been stuck on a plane for ten hours. And, really, shouldn't I be more concerned about running out of water?) Also, left to my own devices, I tend to stock my fridge and pantry to the fullest.

The lie I tell myself is that my safety comes in the form of food (and is it any wonder I've struggled with weight my whole life?). As long as I have something (or a lot of things) with me, I will be OK.

The problem is, I've never starved, so not only do I eat the lunch I buy on the road or at the airport, but also the snacks I've packed for the trip, consuming more calories than a person could ever need.

Since I have a hard time trusting there will ever be enough, it's easy for me to OD on the things that are not healthy for me. Food is my biggest struggle.

Products

I'm talking hair spray, toothpaste, foundation, curl definer, and eyeliner. In my brain, I feel safer if I know that I have a five years' supply of MAC Del Rio lipstick.

I know I also am not a girly girl—I didn't grow up playing with lipsticks or trying to match my blue eye shadow to the color of the sparkles on my sweatshirt. (Remember, I went to high school in the eighties.)

The lie I tell myself is that if I get just the right leave-in conditioner, my hair will finally be bouncy and manageable. If I can just find the right eyeliner, suddenly my dull hazel eyes will pop.

And why not? Advertisers spend millions of dollars to convince you that their product will do it all. I know that we all feel too streetwise to fall for that, but it's amazing how a little bit of exaggeration and a lot of hope will make me try a new product.

Books

For some reason I have this deep-seated fear that I am going to run out of good reading material, so when a new book comes along that interests me, I feel the need to buy it right away.

Office Supplies

Are you like me in that you can't walk by a display of notepads and Sharpie markers without wanting to stock up on everything? I am *addicted* to office supplies. I have Liquid Paper coursing through my veins and I bleed highlighter. I love having reams of paper and stacks of ink cartridges.

The lie I tell myself is that if I have the right tools (the perfect-sized notebook, the pen that feels good in my hand and glides smoothly over the paper,) then I will finally be productive.

What I've come to realize is that this is a scarcity mentality, and it affects more than my stuff.

Trent Hamm, in a post on his blog *The Simple Dollar*, talks about the signs of a scarcity mentality:

> Most people are deeply scripted in what I call the Scarcity Mentality. They see life as having only so much, as though there were only one pie out there. And if someone were to get a big piece of the pie, it would mean less for everybody else.
>
> The Scarcity Mentality is the zero-sum paradigm of life. People with a Scarcity Mentality have a very difficult time sharing recognition and credit, power or profit—even with those who help in the production. They also have a very hard time being genuinely happy for the success of other people.
>
> The Abundance Mentality, on the other hand, flows out of a deep inner sense of personal worth and security. It is the paradigm that there is plenty out there and enough to spare for everybody. It results in sharing of prestige, of recognition, of profits, of decision making. It opens possibilities, options, alternatives, and creativity [Trent Hamm, "Scarcity and Abundance," *The Simple Dollar* (blogpost), October 10, 2010].

Scarcity can show itself in other ways as well.

One time, at a writers conference, I was in a small group of authors who were discussing the challenges of writing. I was honest with the group (perhaps my first mistake) and told them that writing is actually very difficult for me. I failed freshman English, I'm dyslexic, and

I much prefer reading a book than writing one. But I do it because I love to share ideas with others, and my best work never comes easily, so I work hard at writing.

And this totally ticked off another conferee. She looked me square in the eye, pointed a finger at me, and said, "How dare you."

I had no idea what she was talking about. I didn't have to wait long to find out.

"You keep taking book contract after book contract, and you don't even like to write? How could you. You know that there are hundreds of writers out there that *want* to write a book, and every contract you accept, that's another author that can't write a book."

That, my friends, is a scarcity mentality. There are only so many book contracts to go around. Or only so many good jobs. Only so much good fortune. If something good happens for you, your friend can't be happy for you because what it really means is that something good hasn't happened for them.

That is the true definition of a scarcity mentality. If someone else has something I want, that just means less for me. So we hoard and stockpile, collect and keep so that we can control not going without.

How can you tell if your clutter is the result of a scarcity mentality?

- Do you have a hard time controlling yourself when it comes to stocking up on essentials?

- Does your stockpile take up more room than it should?

- Do you find yourself being jealous of what your friends have in their home—wondering why they deserve nice things and you don't?

- Do you have a hard time when your friend gets something that you really want?

How to Fight a Scarcity Mentality

Steven Covey coined the term "abundance mentality" in his book *7 Habits of Highly Effective People*. An abundance mentality says that there is enough for everyone. I can share because there is not a shortage of resource or recognition.

When we actively practice an abundance mentality, we set our hands to share the very things we held on to so tightly in the past: money, things, time, and recognition.

I wrote the following on Facebook after my parents were on the receiving end of someone else's abundance mentality:

> To the couple who ate lunch at Fat City in Sacramento today:
>
> You had no idea that my parents were celebrating my dad's 81st birthday, and that, as much as we wanted to be with them, my family lives far enough away that it wasn't possible. (I'll be there later this week to take them out, but it's not the same as being there on the day.)
>
> So when the waiter told my mom to put away her card because their lunch had been taken care of, my mom didn't know what to make of it. She hadn't told anyone at the restaurant that it was my dad's birthday.
>
> Imagine how surprised she was when the waiter pointed you out and told her you had paid for their lunch. When she went over to you and asked why, you said, "You just seemed like a sweet couple."
>
> Thank you for going out of your way.
>
> Thank you for loving on my parents in person when I couldn't.
>
> Thank you for giving my parents a story that they will remember for the rest of their lives.
>
> Oh, and my husband and I will be doing the same for someone else in honor of you.

Isn't that a beautiful way to live? Trusting that when you feel prompted to share out of your portion, you may be blessing people you don't know or may never meet?

I spoke recently at Silver Spur Conference Center where my former pastor, John, and his wife, Pam, are the directors. Silver Spur lives out the abundance mentality every day. Of every conference center I've ever been to, they serve the best food. They care deeply for the people who are retreating at their center, and while Roger and I were there, the event director, Mona, made sure there were always healthy snacks in our room and that we had camp swag: T-shirts, coffee mugs, refillable water bottles, and more. You have to wonder, where does that come from in a ministry that constantly has to watch its bottom line?

After I spoke one morning, Pam and I were hanging out on the couches in the common room, just talking about life and ministry (my favorite kind of conversation). At some point I told her, "I can't help looking at your earrings. I just love them so much."

After everything I knew about Pam, her husband, and the camp, why was I then surprised that she took those earrings off and handed them to me? I wear those earrings at least twice a week, and each time they are a reminder to me that much of the good things I love and cherish are because of someone else's generous heart toward me.

But that represents only the top layer of Silver Spur's deep abundance mentality. On August 17, 2013, an illegal hunting fire started what was later to be named the Rim Fire in the Sierra Nevada region of California—right in the area of Silver Spur Christian Camps. It is the largest fire on record in the Sierra Nevada.

While the camp was told it may be best to evacuate, Silver Spur didn't shut its doors, though it did cancel upcoming camps for the safety of the campers. Instead, they opened the camp to all the firemen who were working the blaze. Running the camp twenty-four hours a day, camp personnel stayed and served all of those brave firefighters for weeks. They gave them food, rest, and restoration.

As the firefighters would leave camp during the day, the people of the camp, along with their kids, would line up along the road and hold up signs that said things like, "We're Praying for You" and "Be Safe! My House Is Not Worth Your Life!"

That, my friends, is an abundance mentality.

When you live in a world of scarcity, there will never be enough to make you feel safe. Enough food, enough clothes, enough anything. But when you choose a world of abundance, where you are grateful for all that you have and practice that gratitude every single day, your resources will never be so low as you cannot trust the God who provides everything for you that you need.

Some Practical Ways to Practice Abundance

- Make extra for dinner and give it to a neighbor. We do this for our next-door neighbor, who always appreciates it.
- When you buy a Costco-sized anything (toilet paper, soup pack, trash bags), share some of it with a family who is struggling.
- The next time you mow your lawn, ask your elderly neighbor if you can mow hers as well.
- Pack an Operation Christmas Child box with your kids in the midst of your own Christmas shopping.
- Donate food to a food bank and toiletries to a women's shelter.
- Cut your "backups" in half—only two sets of sheets that you use and love instead of six sets that get mixed up and never match.

This is not a "name it and claim it" philosophy. This is the radical understanding that no matter how little we have, we are better when we share.

Part 4

How to Get Rid of Stuff

19

A New Approach to Cleaning Clutter

When my kids were little, they knew the routine before grandparents crossed the threshold of our home. We called it the "Stash and Dash." I didn't care if the house was clean; it just needed to look clean. My thought was, *There is always time to deal with it later.* So laundry baskets would fill up, drawers would get stuffed, closets would get smushed closed, and the house would look clean.

Until my parents left.

And then the first time someone needed to find a pair of shoes or a homework assignment, the entire contents of our house threw up on itself. And that's how our house would stay—until the next time grandma came to visit.

Please say this sounds familiar to you.

I think a lot of us approach clutter this way. We see that a room is cluttered, so we put away everything. We clear off the surfaces and put things in drawers, cabinets, closets, and boxes until the room looks clean. We leave out only those things that are really important because we are afraid if we put it away, we will forget about it or not be able to find it.

Eventually, we need those things that we put away, and we pull them out of our drawers, cabinets, closets, and boxes, and our stuff rises back to the surface.

And our "clean" house is no longer clean.

Or maybe, the truth is that it was never clean to begin with.

After years of this messy cycle, I realized that if I ever wanted my house to be open to drop-in guests (I did), and if I ever wanted to live in a place of sanity instead of a place of stress (I also did that), I needed to find a new way to approach the clutter.

And so I did.

Not right there, not right then, but over time. I thought and prayed and moved and organized, and eventually, I came up with a system that worked for me.

My system is simple (albeit hard) and requires simply four things:

1. Have a safe place to store everything you need.

2. Have enough space to store everything you need.

3. Have a sure way of being able to retrieve those things.

4. Take it one drawer at a time.

The Secret Sauce of Clutter Management

More about this system in a moment, but first let me just say that the real magic of clearing clutter is one simple mind shift: *always look at what you want to keep, not at what you want to get rid of.* Yes, all the tricks in this book will help, but the real magic of this approach is that instead of quickly sorting through a drawer to find out what you want to get rid of, you are carefully and thoughtfully choosing the things you want to keep.

In this way, you are reclaiming your clutter power by carefully choosing to keep the items that you actually love and need and would spend money on again to acquire. I don't know why no one has ever told me this before. This is the secret sauce, people.

Of course, I can give you lots of condiments in addition to the secret sauce, and that's what this section of the book is about—helping you to make wise decisions about what you get rid of and what you decide to keep.

OK, metaphor over. Here's what else I think you need to know.

Ask Yourself the Right Three Questions

What most of us do when we start to attack clutter is to walk into a room, find a drawer to attack, and decide we are going to gut that drawer. We are going to get rid of absolutely everything!

We start going through the drawer and pick up each item, one by one. As we get to the first item, let's say it's a garlic press, we pick it up and start to go through the list of questions in our head:

How much did it cost me?

Who gave it to me?

What will they think if I gave it away?

How much is it worth?

Will I need this someday?

Will I change my mind and want it later on?

These were the questions I used to ask myself when I was trying to decide whether to get rid of something. And since you are someone who struggles with clutter, I'm guessing they are the same questions that rattle around in your mind.

So I look at that garlic press and decide to keep it. Yeah, I have another garlic press—one I like better. But I know this is an expensive one. I'd read about this garlic press on a cooking blog and the author raved about it. It was a life-changing garlic press. So when my friend asked me what I wanted for Christmas, my answer was easy—I wanted the life-changing garlic press. (I even sent her the link from the post I'd read.)

Now as I hold it in my hand, I have to admit it was not a life-changing garlic press. (I shouldn't be surprised. That's a lot of pressure to put on a garlic press.) But what to do?

- I know it was an expensive garlic press.
- My friend gave it to me.

- Maybe my current garlic press will break and I'll need this backup just in case.

- Maybe I'm just not using it correctly. If I only knew the magic secret to using it, it probably would be life-changing.

So instead of making the hard decision to put the garlic press in the donation box, I put it back in the drawer so I can deal with it another day. And that's how a garlic press becomes clutter.

Those questions are not the right questions.

Those questions were getting me into trouble. And I have a feeling they're getting you into trouble too. They muddle decisions and enable you to keep every item whether you want to or not. I needed a better set of clutter questions to help me get unburied from the piles of stuff that were taking over my home. Better questions like these:

1. Do I currently use it?

2. Do I really love it?

3. Would I buy it again?

These three questions? They have become the clarifying lenses I see all my possessions through, and they help me quickly and unemotionally clear the clutter from my life.

The Three Questions in Action

As I'm sitting here on my couch, typing away, I can't help but notice that our coffee table has become cluttered. Here's a list of what's currently on the table:

- two candles

- two remotes

- a bottle of perfume

- a wooden tray

- *Communicating for a Change* (a book someone borrowed and brought back to me yesterday)

- a coffee table book
- four coasters

After quickly surveying the table and asking myself those three questions, I am able to clear the clutter in under three minutes:

- Two candles—I don't currently use, I don't really love these candles, and I wouldn't buy them again. They will go into the donation box.

- Two remotes—Yes, we currently use these, some days more than we should. They get put in the drawer of the coffee table.

- A bottle of perfume—I brought it downstairs to see if my daughter wanted it. She didn't. It goes in the donation box.

- A wooden tray—Roger's dad made this for us and I love it. It stays.

- *Communicating for a Change*—I am not currently using this book, and I don't particularly love looking at it. However, it has changed how I speak and write, and I refer to it periodically. I would pay full price for the book again if my friend had not returned it. It stays.

- A coffee table book—Don't use it, don't love it, wouldn't pay for it (it was a gift). Out it goes.

- Four coasters—We use them daily, Roger's dad made them, and they are beautiful. They stay.

The Things That Pass the Three-Question Test

When cleaning out a drawer, cabinet, or closet, there is something so powerful about pulling out and keeping only those things that you use, love, and would invest in again. I know when I've spent an afternoon pulling out things I'm going to give away, the judge in my head keeps beating me up:

- "You can't give this away! You spent so much money on it!"

- "You can't give that away. What if you need it some day?"

- "Your friend gave you that picture frame. Are you really going to give it to Goodwill?"

Those voices will keep you down in your clutter.

But if you use the three questions, your perspective changes. Instead of getting rid of things, you begin rescuing the things you truly love. You are pulling things off of shelves, out of drawers, out of cabinets that you really love, use, and appreciate. You can gut the rest of the space and give those things to someone who will love them. Notice how the conversation changes:

- "I love this coffee mug. It makes me think of my friend Shane every time I use it."

- "I've read this book four times. Can't wait for reading number five."

- "Yay! Every pair of pajamas in here is my favorite!"

Yes, you are giving away clutter (anything you don't use, love, or wouldn't buy again), but more importantly, you are creating room for the things you value. The things that make it possible to do the work you're called to, the things that remind you of all your people and blessings.

The Half-Empty Principle

One goal I have for my house is to get all my drawers and cabinets half empty so they can be totally functional. You will just continue the clutter cycle if you have overstuffed holding spaces and thus nowhere to put your things.

Here's how I get a drawer to half empty.

Take my pajama drawer. It was, once again, out of control. (Remember, your stuff is a living, breathing organism. Just because you purged it once doesn't mean it's not going to grow out of control again.)

1. The very first step is to utilize the Three-Box, Two-Bag System so that I have a place to put everything. You'll find an explanation of this system in my book *The Get Yourself Organized Project*, but for your convenience, I've also included that material (for free!) in appendix 1 of this book.

2. I pull out the entire contents of my pajama drawer. Most people when organizing pull out the things they know they want to get rid of. But remember, that's backward thinking. Everything I own must earn the right to be there. It must pass the "I use it, I love it, I would buy it again" test. I put the entire contents of my pajama drawer on my bed.

3. Next I put back the "obviously" items. These are my go-to pajamas. These are the ones that pass the "I use it, I love it, I would buy it again" test without even studying. They look great, they feel great, I would work in them all day if it were appropriate. How many pairs are in the "obviously" category? I'm guessing three or four sets of pj's.

4. Then I determine how many pairs of pj's I really need. I'm guessing the number for you may be "obviously" plus one or two. For me, I have three pairs of year-round pj's, two pairs of summer only (shorts and T-shirts), and two pairs of winter only.

5. I put the three "obviously" pairs in the "Put Back" box (see appendix 1) along with the summer pj's (since that's the season we're in as I write this). This is also the box to put any other random clothes (socks, sweats, underwear) that may have gotten put away incorrectly in the pajama drawer. This usually happens when someone else is putting away clothes and doesn't know your system.

6. My winter pj's go in the "Other Rooms" box to be put away with my other winter clothes. (Of course, reverse the "Put Away" and "Other Rooms" contents if you are organizing in winter.)

7. Finally, any pajamas that are not my favorites, don't fit, I don't wear, I wouldn't pay good money for again, go in the "Give Away" box.

8. You need to be ruthless with this box. No "just in case" thinking allowed. (I should hang on to these extra sets "just in case" I don't do laundry for a week, or "just in case" my friend spends the night and needs to borrow them, or "just in case" I lose twenty pounds.) No "but they were a gift" or "they were so expensive" excuses. There is a friend, or maybe someone on a low income, who could desperately use those beautiful, warm, comfortable pajamas, while all they are doing in your drawer is making it hard to put away the clothes you actually use. Being a good steward of your resources means, much of the time, giving those resources away.

9. Any pajamas that are trashed beyond wear? I put those in my garbage or recycling bag. (You should check with your local recycling company to see if they recycle clothing that is beyond respectable wear.)

10. Then I clean out the drawer, wiping it down or vacuuming it out.

11. Finally, I take the "Put Away" box and put away all the clothes in it, whether they are pajamas that go back in the pajama drawer or other clothes that were accidentally hanging out in the pajama drawer.

Now if you've been sorting your pajama drawer along with me, I hope your drawer is about half full, especially since you may still have some pajamas hanging out in the laundry. And that's OK since if they're in the laundry, it means they are ones you wear regularly. If your drawer is more than half full, go through it again and see what you can get rid of.

Trust me. You will not miss any of the pajama clutter (or whatever cluttered drawer or space you are organizing). You know in your head that you didn't love or need any of those extra pajamas. The only time this process will be hard is when you are first getting rid of them. After that, you will never think about those extra pj's again (except to be grateful that someone else is sleeping a little better because of your clearing the clutter).

If you're still worried, try this. Set a reminder on your calendar for two weeks from the day you cleaned out your pajama drawer. Ask yourself, *Do I miss any of those pajamas? Can I even remember what half of them look like?* Probably not.

Now when I open my pajama drawer, I see nothing but things I love to sleep in. I don't have to dig down through all the sloppy seconds. I don't have to wrestle with piles of holey T-shirts. I only see things I love that are going to help me rest.

And that, my friend, is a beautiful thing.

20

Clear Your Decks: The 2000 Things Challenge

W e'll start purging again in January," Robin said. "The goal is for two thousand items to leave the house next year!"

Robin doesn't have any idea how she messed up my life with that one little comment she left on my Facebook page after I posted a picture of twelve bags of good usable clothes and household items we were donating.

But she did.

Because just then I was starting to get really tired of the *things* merry-go-round that seemed to control our house every few months. Every year we accumulate all these things, and every Christmas season we spend days getting rid of stuff right before the holidays when we will (you guessed it) get more stuff to store until the merry-go-round starts again.

But Robin's comment triggered something new in me…and then the insanity took over.

I let myself imagine a home where we only had things that were used, were loved, and we would buy again. Yes! Everything in its place and for a reason and…well, you get it. I'm sure you're imagining the same thing for yourself right now.

I started to dream of being able to give good and valuable things away to those who not only need them but would appreciate them.

And I imagined being free from needless possessions so that if God decides we need to live in Seattle or Denver, we aren't tied down to our stuff.

And the dreaming and imagining lit a fire in me.

I broached the subject carefully with Roger (being the "project" in *The Husband Project*, my husband is used to being subjected to my crazy ideas). He had his concerns.

"Do you really think we can get rid of over two thousand things?"

Um—have you seen our garage? Yes, yes I do.

- 5.5 things a day
- 38 things a week
- 167 things a month

It's a lot. But in the end, after a year, it would be totally worth it.

Are you reading this and feeling the same way? Feeling like you are on the *things* merry-go-round and would do anything to get off that dizzying ride? Are you constantly fighting the influx of things coming in, and then having to deal with getting things out of your house? Are you tired of talking about living simply and want to really feel lighter as the year goes on? Do you want to be able to close your closet and not be afraid the door is going to pop open and attack the next person walking by? Do you want to be able to park a car in your garage?

It doesn't have to be that way. Come…live the dream with us.

I'd like to challenge you to get rid of two thousand things in a year.

Will it be hard? Yes. It was excruciating at times for us. But the trade-offs are totally worth it.

As we went through the weeks and months of culling our possessions, we discovered some interesting things about our stuff (and ourselves):

We were buying convenience.

Instead of finding the guest towels I knew I had, somewhere, I would buy a new set. Instead of thinking ahead and sewing on the button to the jacket I wanted to wear, I'd buy a new jacket. Crazy, right?

We weren't replacing; we were stockpiling.

I hated our broom because it didn't sweep well, so I bought another broom. But instead of getting rid of the bad broom, I just put it in the garage. Why? I hate it. Why keep it?

I owned the most uncomfortable pair of sneakers on the planet. I would have been better off in three-inch stilettos than these "running shoes." But instead of donating those instruments of torture, I put them in the extra closet "just in case."

Just in case what? I ever decided I wanted another reason for foot surgery? Just in case I decide I need to be punished, and uncomfortable shoes are the way to administer it?

For me it was running shoes. For you it may be a can opener that rips your hand every time you use it, or an ugly sweater, or old dish towels to wash your car with. (One friend saved towels for this purpose for ten years and never used one…because she took her car to be washed every two weeks.)

Better planning up front meant less stuff in the long run.

I travel by plane at least thirty times a year. At this point, I feel like packing should be intuitive. But it's not. When I have a list and use it to pack, I know what I brought is what I need. When I don't make a list, I end up making an emergency trip to Target to buy a black tank top or a diffuser for my hairdryer.

We were buying a lot of things because we didn't know what we already had.

"I know we have skewers around here somewhere." "Around here somewhere" is the most common place that people store things. With all the clutter, it's hard to know what you have and what you don't.

The 2000 Things Challenge

So for those of you who have been waiting to get your hands dirty (because, let's face it, some area of your house is just a mess), here's how you get started getting rid of two thousand things:

1. Find two friends (at least) to do this challenge with you.

It doesn't matter if they're phone friends, Internet buddies, or face-to-face girlfriends you meet with at Starbucks down the street. Find someone to keep you accountable.

2. Pick a room—any room—to start the purge.

I would pick the room that's giving you the most stress and start there. You'll feel better when some of the pressure is taken off.

3. Evaluate your plan.

This is where people often give up. If something doesn't work, they will scrap the whole idea. *You* decide what steps you're going to take each day. Then after trying it, see if that is a good goal. Feel free to change it, but just keep your focus on trying to organize areas of your life.

4. Be flexible.

The intention of the 2000 Things Challenge is not to add stress, but to make your life simpler by removing the clutter from your life and helping you stay organized. Just do something, intentionally, every day. If you can be flexible in the day-to-day goals, you will learn to be flexible when things come up that you cannot control. And in this way, we are no longer purging just clutter from our homes, but also the clutter of disappointment or anxiety if something doesn't go perfectly in our life. Because let's be real. Life on earth is not perfect. But we do have a perfect God who will help us get through it!

5. Come up with some ground rules.

First you need some ground rules, especially if you and your spouse don't see eye-to-eye on the types of things that are "necessary" to running a house. Which means that if he can't throw away your yoga pants that have holes in the seams, then you can't throw away his recliner that has been decorating your house since you got married. You both have to be in it together.

Here are the rules that we set up for our house:

- Consumables are not counted. (Doggy waste bags don't count—the plastic doggy-waste-bag holder does.)

- If a piece of a set can be used on its own, it's counted. (For example, each piece of silverware counts, but a thousand-piece puzzle counts as one thing.)

- We will donate or get rid of things in the most responsible way possible.

- We will work together to be thoughtful and intentional in the process so no one is upset.

Some Tips for the 2000 Things Challenge

Here are some tips that helped me get through as I got rid of two thousand things:

1. Have a Donation Station.

One of the difficulties I encountered during the 2000 Things Challenge was keeping track of all the things I came across that I knew I didn't need anymore. I needed a dedicated place to put those things (that also had easy access) until I could count and donate them.

Finally, I cleaned out a small portion of our closet in the office and put a box in there lined with a large garbage bag. Every time I found something that I no longer needed or wanted, it went to the closet. Once the bag was full, I counted the things and then put the bag in my car to donate.

If your Donation Station is in your garage or basement, you are less likely to put things away there. Instead, put your Donation Station somewhere that you will see it every day. Let it be a constant reminder to you and your family that you are getting rid of two thousand things. (Feel free to hide it when company comes over.)

2. Take time to purge every day.

This goes without saying, but if you wait until December to start getting rid of two thousand things, you might struggle a little bit. Instead, do your best to get rid of a few things every day. Here are a few ideas to get you started:

- Go through your magazine rack and pitch any issue that's over three months old.
- Go through your gadget drawer in your kitchen.
- If it's spring or summer, donate any clothes you didn't wear all winter, as well as any summer clothes that you're pulling out that just don't work for you anymore.
- Do the same with your kids' clothes.
- If it's fall or winter, donate any clothes you didn't wear all summer…(you get the idea).
- Look at the paperwork on your desk. Every decision is a thing and it counts.

3. Keep count (even if you don't feel like it).

There is something about totaling up the number of items that keeps you focused. You want to get to that next hundred (or thousand), and setting intermediate goals is a good way to keep you reaching for that next number.

Two thousand things seems like an overwhelming number, but I've never had anyone say they couldn't do it. Start small (a hundred things) and get the feel for processing your stuff. You'll feel lighter in less than a day.

I promise.

21

Adopt a Uniform

When I was growing up, my mom would tell me tales about when she worked at Kline's department store in Kansas City as a high schooler. She loved her job because she loved clothes and would put most of her paycheck directly back into the store. She told me how she would stock up on stockings and skirts and blouses, and I loved imagining her outfits and picturing her in them.

But what I loved most about her stories was what she said about the very strict dress code for the women. Back in her day, the very exciting fashion color choices were:

- black
- brown
- gray
- navy blue

And, just to throw in a little spice, they were allowed to wear a white shirt. I know…pretty daring, right?

That's what my mom had to wear. Not very exciting, right? And I wonder how she was such a clothing fanatic with so few choices. But she was. And if I really think about it, there's something inside of me that craves the simplicity of a dress code.

No, I don't want to be forced to wear the same thing every day, but I also love the simplicity of having a few choices that I know look good on me and will make me feel confident when I go out.

I used to buy clothes that I thought were cute without thinking about anything else. A cute pair of shorts on sale? Sure. Who cares that I hate wearing shorts and always feel uncomfortable in them. A nice T-shirt in a lovely shade of yellow? Awesome. Never mind that yellow isn't my best color. And then the clothes would sit in drawers and closet unworn, and I'd wonder why my drawers and closet were so disorganized.

There had to be a better way.

And after considering this for a while, I came to the conclusion that anyone who wants to cut clutter and simplify her life needs to have her own version of the uniform. For example, my summer wardrobe for work consists of:

- linen or cotton pants or a maxi-skirt in white, cream, black, brown, chambray
- cotton shirts or T-shirts
- cotton or linen jackets or a lightweight sweater
- two-inch wedge sandals
- a chunky necklace

My summer wardrobe for days off is the same, just swap out the linen pants for jeans or cotton cargo pants and replace the heels for flats, and I'm ready to rock 'n' roll.

My assistant, Kim Nowlin, always looks like she stepped off the pages of *Lucky*. She always looks amazing. But when you break it down, 75 percent of the time she's wearing jeans, flats, a T-shirt, and a chunky necklace. (Which is awesome, by the way, when she shows up to my house and I'm in my yoga pants. And it's 10:30.) I doubt that she's ever worn the same outfit to my house twice. But the pieces of the outfits? Yep—they've made appearances over and over again.

Following Kim's example, I've started doing the same thing. I buy only certain styles of clothes and I don't buy many of them.

This week I just got back from an eight-day trip to Georgia. The first few days were to spend some time with Roger's family, and the last several days were a business trip where I was going to be meeting with publishers, agents, fellow authors, and speakers. I brought my whole summer wardrobe with me. When I travel in the winter for a week, I bring my whole winter wardrobe with me, except for one outfit (so I have something to wear the day I get home). I don't have extras because clothes I don't wear are clutter I don't need.

Plus, when I think about the woman who would lovingly wear the white eyelet laced shirt I have hanging in my closet (but I don't wear because it washes me out so much I look like a cast member on *True Blood*), I start to realize that keeping clothes I don't need is a pretty selfish way to live.

How to Get Down to a Minimalist Wardrobe

1. Inventory everything you have.

Most of us don't even know what's hiding in our closets. Sure, we know what the top ten items are (because those are the ones we constantly wear, put in the laundry, and then put away). But when you dig everything out, I'm guessing you'll be able to get rid of 25 percent of your stuff right off the bat.

Stop playing the game of, "Well, if I run out of all my good clothes, I still have this shirt that I don't like that I could wear in an emergency." There is no need. You will never run out of clothes. Why wear something that you don't like?

If you do like it but don't wear it for other reasons, do not put it back in your closet. Maybe it doesn't fit quite right or it needs to be repaired. Put it by the front door to take to the drycleaner or the tailor, go get the seam ripper and remove the scratchy tag, mix up a batch of super stain remover and soak it to get rid of that stain. But do not put it back in your closet where it goes from clothing to clutter simply because you would never wear it in its present condition.

2. Make a packing list.

So many times I've walked around with the vague notion that I don't have the right clothes for an event, for work, or for a weekend away. So what's a middle-class American to do? Wander into a mall and buy something "perfect" for just such an occasion. Oh, how many times have I wasted time and money doing just that?

But chances are, I had the perfect (or almost perfect) thing in my wardrobe all along, but I just didn't remember it or plain couldn't find it.

One of the best things you can do when you have a trip coming up (and for your wardrobe in general) is to make a packing list a week or so before hitting the road. This will do several things for you:

- It will get you over the vague notion that you have nothing to wear.
- It will make your packing day a breeze.
- It makes sure everything is "pack ready."
- When you are just throwing things into a suitcase the night before, inevitably that favorite silky T-shirt that goes with all your work clothes or that favorite pair of palazzo pants will be at the bottom of your dirty clothes hamper. And then you either have to go without or sit up until 1:30 in the morning to make sure that everything is clean and ready for your 6:30 flight the next morning.
- You are way less likely to forget a certain belt or necklace.

(Or worse—all your underwear. While you're at Disneyland. On your honeymoon. Stranded without a car. And it takes you two days to find the store that sells Tinker Bell briefs because you're too embarrassed to ask. Been there.)

Packing well will keep you from buying things you don't need and will keep your suitcase and your closet less cluttered.

Here are a few more ideas for reducing the size of your wardrobe:

- Put things you're not sure about in an extra closet and attach to each item a date by which you have to decide to keep it or give it away.

- Write a list of the types of clothes you wear and where you buy them so you're not tempted to buy things on a whim.

- Keep wardrobes in sections in your closet—top shelf is "summer wardrobe," bottom is "winter wardrobe," and anything that doesn't fit into one of your wardrobes gets donated.

- It may be worth it to work once with a stylist (or a really talented friend) who can help you narrow down your needs and help you purge what doesn't work or doesn't flatter.

I'm not trying to take away anyone's clothing fun. But one thing I've noticed about Kim and all the other stylish women I know: they don't have a ton of clothes. The clothes they do have are ones they love, that fit them well, and that they wear over and over.

Find the fun not in shopping for new clothes to fall in love with but in falling in love with the clothes you already own and figuring out new ways to wear them. Your closet will thank you.

22

Use It Up

U*se it up, wear it out, make it do, or do without.*
    I know certain people like to complain that they had to walk uphill to school both ways as kids. (Not me, of course. I rode my Schwinn Rainbow bike uphill both ways.) But back in the day, our grandmothers really did have it rough.

During the war, everything from socks to sugar to meat to (gasp!) coffee was rationed. Which meant everyone had to do without and do without a lot. Have you read *Guernsey Literary and Potato Peel Pie Society*? If not, you totally should and if so, do you remember what they had to live off of? They made pie out of potato peels. And called it dessert!

And while I'm not about to give up my mocha gelato (even in the name of decluttering), I do think we have something to learn from this. Back during World War II, one of the most popular mottos was "Use it up, wear it out, make it do, or do without." And a tiny part of me thinks we should start bringing that back.

Use It Up

In January, I gave myself a challenge: Could I go six months without buying any cosmetics, hair products, bath products, toothpaste, toothbrushes, or other personal care products?

Now before you assume that I had an aggressive disregard for personal hygiene, I want to assure you that smelling good is a pretty important priority in my life, and I am very fond of my teeth.

My problem was that my bathroom clutter had taken on a life of its own. I had hair products coming out my follicles, nail polishes and skin buffers galore, and enough cosmetics to start my own little MAC counter.

I did a little archaeological digging through all of my personal-care products and tried to uncover the reason why I'm addicted to this stuff. In the process, I learned a few things about myself:

- I am a hair product junkie. I will buy anything that anyone recommends to control my red frizzy hair. Apparently money (and storage space) is no object.

- I forget to replenish my supplies. Which is one of the reasons why, when I travel, I've had to make late-night trips to get the right shampoo in the middle of Canton, Georgia.

- I'm addicted to Costco. So I don't buy one tube of toothpaste, I buy six. Even if I just bought six the last time I went to Costco four weeks ago.

- I don't know how to throw away virtually empty bottles.

- I don't know how to use the last tenth of a product so that the bottle is empty.

- I don't know how to throw away products that cause severe allergic reactions.

- I don't know how to throw away gifts that someone gave me, even if the smell makes me slightly queasy.

- I can't pass up a hotel shampoo, conditioner, lotion, or mouthwash.

All of these clutter traps led me to a life of wading through products to get to what I really need. It was really and truly out of control.

So I put myself on a six-month, product-buying sabbatical. Here were my rules:

1. I would use up all the products in my house until they were gone or the six months were up. Whichever came first. So if I ran out of face cleaner before the six months was up, I could buy new face cleaner. But if I still had some (but just didn't like the smell of it), I either had to throw it away or use it up.

2. If I didn't want to use that almond body butter, then I needed to throw it away.

3. Only when I was completely out of a product could I go buy some more. That meant if I was going to buy shampoo, I had to use up any old bottles, hotel bottles, and off brands. If I wasn't going to use them, I needed to dump them or pass them on before I bought any new products.

It was a simple challenge, but it wasn't easy. Whenever I'd get my hair done, my stylist had a new product I had to try. When I traveled, I had to make sure that I had all my products with me—no emergency trips to Target to get hair spray.

But once those six months were up, my stash of products was much smaller and I had only those items that I truly use and love. Plus, I didn't spend one dime on products. (Yes, I still got my hair cut and spent money to maintain my redhead status, but there are some things a girl cannot compromise on.)

Use it up, wear it out, make it do, or do without is a great principle, not only for saving money but also for decreasing clutter in our lives.

In a Los Angeles study of the buying habits of thirty-two families, researchers noticed over and over again that these families would purchase a new item but often fail to get rid of the item they were replacing. They wanted to keep the old item in order to put it on Craigslist or sell at a garage sale, since it was still in working order.

What if we were to purchase things with the thought in mind that we would replace it only when it was beyond repair?

What if we used our products completely up instead of getting tired of one lotion and replacing it with another?

What if, instead of running to Bed Bath & Beyond to buy a heart-shaped cupcake pan in order to make heart cupcakes for our daughter's fifth grade class, we googled how to make heart-shaped cupcakes with the pan we have? (Put a marble between each cupcake liner and the cupcake pan to bend the cupcake into a heart shape as it bakes.)

Or what if we didn't make heart-shaped cupcakes at all and just made regular cupcakes that the kids were going to devour in less than ninety seconds anyway.

Wear It Out

We have become a nation of replacers, not repairers.

When our shoes get scuffed we toss them out instead of getting them repaired (or sometimes, even just shining them).

Instead of sewing on a stray button, we go buy a new shirt. My daughter had a college friend who threw away a pair of running shoes because she didn't know you could buy replacement shoelaces.

Instead of replacing items, what if we took the time to refurbish them. Buy things for the long haul. Instead of buying patterned dishes (and growing tired of them after a couple of years,) buy plain ones and mix and match them with what you already have.

Buy furniture with the knowledge that it's going to acquire a few scratches and dents along the way.

I want my house to look not only lived in, but loved in. And that means resisting the urge to replace all the time.

Make It Do

I know I'm going to start sounding like your old crotchety grandfather right now, but keeping your old things is a lot cheaper than buying new. I know my mom used to always talk to me about things like "proper car maintenance" and "regular oil changes" and "not pressing so hard on the brake just because you think you saw a squirrel." It may have sounded like one of the adults in a *Peanuts* animated cartoon ("whah wa whah wa wa") when I was younger, but now I know the wisdom in it. Because if my car—my totally paid for car—lasts a year longer than it would if I wasn't maintaining it, then it's worth the trouble. And the truth is that if we take care of our things, then we not only save the trouble and cost of buying new, but we have nicer things to use when we need them.

Here are some simple hacks to help make the things you have last:

- Hang dry your nice sweaters and dresses so they don't get worn out from constant heating and cooling in the dryer.

- Use only a dime size of shampoo or body wash (it says so on the bottle!) and use a sponge or washcloth to rub it in.

- Let your kids wear their nice shoes only to school and church. At home, get a cheap pair of flip-flops or sneakers for them to wear in the mud.

- Set the table with mismatched china or pieces from multiple sets for special occasions. It will look shabby chic (which in case you didn't know, is code word for "totally cool").

Do Without

My husband and I are taking "do without" to the extreme. We are about to go down to one car. My minivan (which is fifteen years old and has been on the "make it do" plan for the past six years) got back from our trusty auto mechanic, who told my husband, "I've known you for a long time, so it's even harder to give you the bad news, but it's the transmission. Your van has only so many more miles to go." Fixing the transmission on a fifteen-year-old car is like buying curtains for the hotel room you're staying one night in—it's a bad investment and it doesn't make a whole lot of sense.

We knew this day would come, so about five years ago we started saving up for a new car. But as the end drew nearer and nearer, the idea of replacing the car became less and less appealing.

I work from home 90 percent of the time. The other 10 percent? Most of that is airplane travel. I do very little travel by car. And since Roger works from home two days a week, and doesn't work on weekends, there is a car available to me four days a week.

So now I'm purposely not driving my minivan in order to make it last as long as possible.

Will I survive without a car? Yes. Will I decide after six months that adding a second car back into our lives is necessary for the health of our marriage? Perhaps. But we are doing something we've never done before. We're asking the question, Can we do without a second car?

Not every one of these strategies is going to work all the time or for every family. But I want us to be intentional about our stuff. And I want us to think through when we can postpone the purchase of a book (or a car, or a house, or a...)

Think of this as a game. How long can I go without buying hair products? Can I make that roll of paper towels that normally lasts a week stretch to two? The grand prize? More money in your account and less clutter in your life.

23

If You Don't Know It Exists, You Will Never Miss It

My friend Erin is an enabler. I often stay at her house when I'm traveling to Austin, Texas, and she just has *the cutest stuff.* (I suspect we all have at least one friend like her.) Now Erin doesn't have a problem with stuff. Me? Yeah—just give me an excuse to buy something (It just went on sale! They are running low on stock! It's in my size!), and I can hit "Place this item in my basket" faster than you can say "for a limited time only!"

So when Erin started sending me the web addresses of some flash sales of things she thought would look cute on me, well, my resistance was low.

So I signed up for their emails. What harm could it do? Maybe I'd find the perfect outfit. You know the one—it's totally comfortable for me to wear all day working at the house and then magically looks super cute to wear out to dinner with my husband.

(Of course, the perfect outfit doesn't exist. Sure, you could have a cute and comfortable thing to wear, but if you're like me, you have an 80 percent chance of either spilling lunch on your shirt or having some living creature—dog, cat, small child—who will guarantee that you are a mess even before you hit the town with your hottie. You always have to change clothes. Always.)

We sign up for the email thinking there's no harm in it. Until the email tells you in no uncertain terms that maxi-skirts are the hottest thing ever and your summer won't be complete without one (or six). That is, until next season when miniskirts are the must have and what were you thinking buying that maxi-skirt last year?

That company is sending you an email for one reason and one reason only: They want you to buy something right now you hadn't thought of buying ten minutes ago. If you unsubscribe from that email, your chances of buying that item go down to 0 percent.

Reactive shopping is big business today. Think about it. As little as a dozen years ago, companies' most direct ways of getting at you were through ads in newspapers and magazines, on radio and TV, and through the mail. Now we are allowing these companies into our inboxes with little "Buy Now" buttons sitting right next to the item. It used to be that we had to get in the car and drive to the store to find the item. Now, with the click of a button, we can have the item in our house in two days and not even have to change out of our yoga pants.

So when a project at work gets too hard, we click on over to our email and buy that chevron blouse or bubble necklace that makes us feel like it will instantly pull the rest of our ragtag wardrobe together. And then we have one more piece of clothing or jewelry or pair of shoes to manage.

And don't even get me started on spinoff purchases. You know when you buy those cute shoes, but they are the wrong height for the pair of pants you were going to wear them with, so instead of returning them...(Because let's be honest, that's a hassle and nine times out of ten, the item will sit in your car in a plastic bag for months. Not that I know that from experience or anything.)

Some of you are thinking right now, *I don't have junk in my house. I only have good stuff that I love!* The problem—you might not even know what you have because you really can have too much of a good thing.

If we are going to war with our clutter, one of the ways we are letting the enemy infiltrate our camp is by the advertisements that we allow to enter our home. What can we do to keep these things at bay?

Unsubscribe.

Use the unsubscribe button liberally. Yes, you ordered a pair of shoes from that cute online store and saved five dollars using the discount they sent you because you're an email subscriber. But now you've paid that five dollars over and over again by giving them access to your email account. And suddenly, you didn't know that you needed that cute boho top until that email popped up in your inbox.

Take flyers straight to the recycling bin.

Take a step back.

Anytime you put something in your checkout cart online, force yourself to step away for at least twenty-four hours. It will almost certainly still be there the next day (and if it's not, then it wasn't meant to be), and it will temper the impulsivity of the purchase.

Press "don't save my credit card information" in the payment section so you have to reenter the numbers every time. This gives you a bit of time to let reality sink in.

To increase your resistance to advertising efforts to persuade you to buy, force yourself to get rid of or sell a new article of clothing every time you buy one. So one new maxi-skirt means one old one to Goodwill.

Set limits on your wardrobe and your kids' wardrobes by making a list of the items you truly need and posting it in a place where you will see it often. For example, here is Erin's list:

I need:

- five pairs of shorts
- four pairs of jeans
- one pair of black pants
- four dresses

- four skirts
- four sweaters

Anything above that, she gives away.

If I worked in an office, I would make sure I had fourteen shirts and seven bottoms (pants, skirts) that I could mix and match. Since I work mainly from home, with travel thrown in where I have to look like a capable human being, I have ten shirts and five bottoms that I can mix and match for a number of different looks.

But I know this because I know what I have. And it keeps me from drooling over Pinterest or the Nordstrom catalog because I know what I have is enough.

When you have enough and you know it, you can trash that catalog and you can skip over the ads in those magazines. You don't have to cut out the coupons because 20 percent off of something you don't need suddenly isn't so appealing.

Enough is a beautiful thing.

24

50 Things to Get Rid of Today

Sometimes the first step to decluttering is actually taking a step. And so to start, I came up with this list of things you can get rid of right now. Today.

1. *Other people's stuff*

You are not someone else's storage unit. If clutter is an issue in your life, one of the first things you must do to recover is to stop enabling others. Your grown children need to come get their stuff. If they live across the country, and have boxes upon boxes stored at your house, ask them to tell you what items they want, and you can send them to them.

If they are local, do what we did with our son Jeremy. We gave his six boxes a move-out date. To Goodwill. At 11:30 on the night of the move out, Jeremy was in our garage, wading through boxes. After four years of storing things, he took exactly twelve items from his boxes. We got our shelves back.

2. *Magazines*

I have a couple of magazine subscriptions that I still hold on to because they are free and I read them each month. But I give myself a time limit to read each issue (the month that's still on the cover), and then I walk the expired issues over to my neighbor. She shares a free subscription with me, and I don't have the paper clutter lingering in my house. If you want to save a particular recipe or article for future reference, snap a picture of it. Try the free app Keepy for a super high-tech way to save precious papers.

3. *Extra food*

People are reluctant to give up food because "I paid good money for it." But if your pantry is so stuffed that you don't know what you have anymore, it is costing you money because you are most likely rebuying ingredients you don't need. Clear it out and donate the nonperishables that aren't past their "best by" date to a local food bank, an adult child, or a friend who has fallen on hard times.

4. *Duplicates*

Remember back in the old days when you didn't know what you had because you had too much clutter, so you bought a wok because, even though you knew you had one somewhere, you couldn't find it (and then found it two weeks later under some tablecloths in the basement)? Well, it's time to give that second wok away.

5. *Guilt gifts*

Get rid of anything that anyone gave you that you don't love.

6. *Any toy from the Dollar Store*

'Nuff said.

7. *Any toy from a Happy Meal*

8. *Anything that doesn't have all of its parts*

Puzzles, toys, games, crafts. If it's just missing one part and it can be replaced, go online and order the missing part or contact the manufacturer. If you are planning to wait until you have time, someday, then just get rid of it now. Someday will never come.

9. *"Just in case" items*

You know that pair of high-waisted mom jeans you're hanging on to "just in case"? (Just in case they come back into fashion or you need them for an eighties party or all your other clothes are dirty.) Pitch 'em.

10. *Your child's artwork*

Again, take a picture with an app like Keepy and then throw it away.

11. *You child's homework or school project*

12. *Things that need to be fixed*

If you've held on to that purse for a year because a buckle needs to be repaired, those pants need to be hemmed, or that vacuum needs to go into the shop, either take it this week or get rid of it. Give yourself a deadline to make it happen so that it will stop being clutter and start being useful.

13. *Cards*

Whenever I receive a card, I put it up on my red hutch to look at for a while. But how long are you supposed to have the card on display in your house? And when it's time to take it down, am I supposed to save it or throw it away? Reminds me of this scene from a *Seinfeld* episode:

> *Kristin*: You got the card I sent?
>
> *Jerry*: I did.
>
> *Kristin*: So where is it?
>
> *Jerry*: What?
>
> *Kristin*: The card. Is this it in the trash?
>
> *Jerry*: No.
>
> *Kristin*: This is my card, you threw it away.
>
> *Jerry*: Well—
>
> *Kristin*: I put a lot of thought into this card.
>
> *Jerry*: You signed your name and you addressed the envelope, it's not like you painted the picture and wrote the poem.
>
> *Kristin*: Fine. I gotta get back to the office.
>
> *Jerry*: Why, because I threw the card out? How long was I supposed to save it?

Kristin: You have no sentimentality.

Jerry: I have sentimentality, really, I'm sentimental. Here, look. Here's some cards I've saved, these are birthday cards from my grandmother, see, I'm not a bad guy.

Kristin: Oh, so you save her cards but not mine! Oh great!

New scene. Jerry and George are at the coffee shop.

Jerry: It was a thank-you card from Kristin because I'm doing the PBS drive. I mean, how long am I supposed to keep it?

George: The rule is a minimum of two days.

Jerry: You making that up or do you know what you're talking about?

George: I'm making it up.

14. *Stained clothes*

Yes, you are allowed to give it one more shot with the miracle stain remover your sister found on Pinterest. After that, it's time to recycle or throw away.

15. *Extra toilet paper rolls, egg cartons, juice can lids, empty pudding cups, clean meat trays, or anything else you've been stashing for art projects*

If you have an art project in mind (and are the kind of person who actually does art projects), you have my permission to keep as many as you will need for the project. Otherwise, recycle what you can.

16. *Potted plants*

If you have a black thumb and plants die on you all the time, you have my permission to give them away to someone who isn't a plant murderer.

17. *Printer cartridges*

For printers you don't even own anymore? Get rid of them.

18. *Any tool or component for something you don't own anymore*

This goes for those little Allen wrenches, gadgets, gizmos, whatever.

19. *Spare buttons that come in little plastic bags on clothes*

Are you really going to sew the button onto the sweater that you probably donated three years ago?

20. *Books*

I'm a huge bookworm and I completely condone keeping as many books as you think you'll read or use again. But if it's something you probably will never pick up again, then donate it.

21. *Cookbooks*

Same goes for cookbooks. If you never open it, you will probably never cook from it.

22. *Mugs*

I use the same three coffee mugs every day. And thus the "I heart New Mexico" mug that has been sitting at the back of my cabinet for three years collecting dust needs to find a new home.

23. *Well-loved pet toys*

Yes, you may get the urge to carefully scrub the grime off the pet toy with a toothbrush and to whip out a needle and thread to sew the hole your dog chewed in it. But most likely, it just needs to be tossed.

24. *Well-loved towels*

Once a dish or bath towel starts to get grungy, you're not going to use it anyway, are you? So toss it. Save a few as rags and get rid of the rest.

25. *Home décor that doesn't fit your style anymore*

That light-blue ceramic goose that you bought in 1992 to go with your ceramic farmhouse collection? Yeah, it's not going to come back into style, and you are no more likely to decorate your mantel with ceramic farm animals now than you were then.

26. *Picture frames*

Just like the ceramic goose, some frames go out of style. Take out the picture and put it in an album for posterity and donate the frame.

27. *Stuffed animals*

Does your kid really need 2,234 stuffed animals to keep her company at night? Have her choose her 6 favorites and donate the rest.

28. *Mismatched socks*

No, the sock monster isn't going to appear with the match to all the missing socks you've been storing for years. Toss them.

29. *Old undies*

Likewise, there is a time and a place for old underwear—you know, the ones with holes in them that you wear only when all the other pairs are dirty. And that time is now and that place is in the garbage.

30. *Your husband's old undies (see above)*

31. *DVDs that you haven't watched in more than a year*

Yes, I get that the retro copy of *The Parent Trap* is sentimental, but if you haven't watched it in a year, then you should probably donate it. No use taking up shelf space for something you'll never watch again.

32. *VHS tapes and cassette tapes*

As a general rule of thumb, if you don't have the device to watch or listen to something, then you probably shouldn't own it.

33. *Old bedding*

I stored the comforter I used on my twin bed as a girl for something like twenty years "just in case" I ever wanted to use it again. Well, guess what? My taste for Rainbow Bright room décor still hasn't resurrected itself, and the comforter is so grungy that I can't imagine sleeping under it anyway.

34. *Shoes that hurt your feet*

I know they are cute. I know they would look great with your blue skirt. But if they hurt, you will never wear them. Donate them.

35. *Old cell phones*

Keep one working in case of emergencies? Yes. Six? No way.

36. *Old cell-phone accessories*

If it's more than three years old, no one wants it. Promise.

37. *"Free" cups from amusement parks*

I know you paid seventeen dollars for the refillable cup, but you don't get free refills at your house. Let it go.

38. *Pictures of people you don't like*
    Just because you are related doesn't mean that person's photo needs to be in your house.

39. *Old curtains*
    If you buy a bigger house, you are not going to want to hang old curtains in it.

40. *Uncomfortable bras*
    I hereby give you permission, no matter how much you spent on them. Pitch them.

41. *Old prescription glasses*
    Keep one for emergencies and donate the others.

42. *Old computer parts*

43. *Old phone systems*

44. *Any free pens that you've received (or accidentally stolen)*
    Cheap pens are cheap for a reason.

45. *Any piece of furniture you don't use and you don't love no matter how much you paid for it*

46. *Flat pillows*
    Life is too short.

47. *Candleholders*
    Because, let me guess, you've been given a dozen as gifts. You can't love them all.

48. *Anything that has been stuck to your fridge for more than a year*

49. *Those keys that've been on your ring for over three years and you don't know what they go to*

50. *Anything with the name of a city on it*

25

50 Ways to Reduce the Stuff Coming into Your Life

Now that you've read through the previous chapter and gotten rid of fifty things (you did do that, right?), another step on your journey to becoming clutter free is to keep unnecessary stuff from coming into your life in the first place. Here are some ideas of ways you can do that.

1. *Encourage non-thing gifts.*

Tell the people you know and love what make great gifts and which ones are harder for you to use and love. Yes, there are probably some physical, tangible things that you would use and love, but give your family the freedom to think outside the box. Some of the gifts we've encouraged are

- perishables (we love home-baked goods)
- gift cards (there's nothing wrong with a Starbucks gift card or an iTunes download)
- experiences (going out to dinner together or at each other's homes)
- just spending time together

This Christmas, my daughter Kimberly gave my parents a day of labor. Kimber offered to go to my parents' house a couple hours away and help them clean and organize their garage. It was a great way to give a gift when Kimber was short on money, and my mom appreciated it way more than any trinket Kim could have bought them.

My sweet kids know about my clutter-free quest and did their part to support me this past birthday. Justen and Kimberly got me a beautiful necklace made out of seeds. I absolutely love it and wear it almost every day. (I gave another necklace to Goodwill the same week.) They went in together on one special thing they knew I would love instead of a lot of little things I didn't need. I loved the intention behind the gift and the fact that they wanted to help me keep my stuff under control.

My stepdaughter and her boyfriend got me a pound of my favorite coffee, and my stepson got me a beautiful bouquet of flowers in my favorite colors.

2. *Buy e-books instead of hardback or paperback.*

I especially love fiction and memoir—anything that's story based—in an e-book version. Some people balk at this and say, "I just love the feel of a book in my hands." That's fine, but if you are struggling with clutter, part of the reason may be that you are not willing to think about ways to reduce the clutter because you are stuck in old patterns. For you, is it about reading a book or how reading a book makes you feel? At first it was hard for me to get used to an e-book, but now it's my preferred way of reading. I can pull out my phone while I'm waiting at the doctor's office or I'm stuck in line at the DMV and pick up where I left off. I don't even have to be prepared: my books now follow me wherever I go.

3. *Listen to audiobooks or other book downloads.*

I am a big audiobook lover. I love to listen to books while I'm cleaning house, walking the dog, cooking dinner, and driving. Instead of buying physical books, get an Audible.com membership and download books to your phone.

4. *Use reusable k-cups.*

I love my Keurig—one cup of coffee at a time. But not only did having all those disposable cups ready and waiting take up a lot of space, they also cost a load of money. Now I have four reusable k-cups that I fill up every couple of days with my favorite coffee (bought on sale, of course). They take up a lot less space than the Costco-sized box of disposable cups and save me a ton of money. Yes, they take one extra minute if you fill them each morning, but if you're an experienced Keurig user, you know that this is about the same amount of time it takes for the water to heat up.

5. *Just say no to souvenirs.*

Get out of the souvenir mindset every time you go someplace new—especially with kids. As a former sales rep in the gift industry, I am guilty of setting up those displays with personalized bracelets and teddies with theme park T-shirts at every tourist trap within a hundred miles of my house. They have you right where they want you. Begging kids, tired parents. It's a deadly mix.

When Roger and I took our kids on a once-in-a-lifetime trip, we set up some souvenir ground rules ahead of time: We would buy each kid and ourselves one shirt, but each of us had to get rid of a shirt when we got home.

And then Roger saw some tall glasses he really liked. But I was on board with that because we desperately needed some new glasses (both Roger and I had been going through a clumsy phase and we were down to three). But there was a plan and a purpose in each of those souvenirs. We still have all of them and use those glasses every day.

6. *Get off of mailing lists.*

Register at www.directmail.com/junk_mail to get off those mailing lists.

7. *Redo Christmas.*

Try doing a stuff-less Christmas with part of your family. You may decide that the adults are not going to exchange gifts (after discussing with the other adults, of course) but will go in on an experience together instead. My mom told me two years ago that she didn't want any more stuff for the house. That has forced me to get creative about what I can do for her and my dad. Now I do things like gift cards to their favorite eateries, flowers, plants for their garden, or movie tickets.

Last Christmas my mom made me and each of our girls four fabric shopping totes. Did she give us stuff? Yes, but those shopping totes have saved us money (we are charged per grocery bag where I live) and stuff (no bags coming into our house). And as a bonus, my mom used up part of her fabric stockpile for quilting, which helped reduce the craft clutter in her life.

8. *Go to Target (or wherever your weakness lies) less often.*

Target is a tough store for me to go to now that I'm striving for a clutter-free life. If I'm going there for groceries, it's so easy to get sucked into the home goods section for a cute pillow or dishtowel. For me, it's better to go less often and then...

9. *Shop with a list.*

When I have a list of exactly what I need, I am way less likely to stroll into aisles I have no business being in. I try to make a game out of shopping—if I have ten things on my list, can I make it to the checkout aisle in less than ten minutes without bodychecking anyone?

10. *Love your library.*

Yes, it's a great way to watch DVDs and try out books without having them permanently in your home, but now many libraries loan items you may not have even considered. After the Oakland Hills fire in 1991, the local library started a resource center to help the victims of that devastating fire. Part of that offering was a tool-lending library that has more than five thousand items that can be checked out as easily as borrowing the latest Stephen King novel.

11. *Be neighborly.*

Exactly how many times are you going to use that wok this year? Once? Twice? How many times will your neighbor use theirs? If you are close enough with your neighbors, offer to let them use something that would enhance their life—lend them your tent for their next camping trip, or your barbecue grill for their next family cookout. That way, you will already have a deposit of good will the next time you want to borrow their weed whacker.

12. *Refuse the hanger.*

When you buy a new article of clothing, just say no to the hanger. Wire or otherwise.

13. *Keep it simple.*

I used to be the kind of mom who wanted to decorate for every single holiday—Christmas, Easter, Fourth of July, it didn't matter. I wanted coordinating plates for every occasion. Until I realized I either had to clear away all the clutter in order to decorate or just decorate on top of the junk.

I still like to decorate, but I keep it much simpler. Now that my life has gotten a little simpler and less cluttered, so has my decorating for holidays. My plates? I have a dozen clear glass plates that I bought for two dollars each at IKEA ten years ago, and they go with everything for every holiday.

14. *Do a seasonal switch-out.*

Instead of a major preholiday shopping trip and later declutter, keep four bins in your garage or attic, one for each season. In them, keep treasured items for winter, spring, summer, and fall, and each season, swap out the next bin and mix the seasonal stuff in with your tried-and-true standbys.

15. *Think permanent.*

Instead of scented candles (which never, ever get used up in my house), try a Scentsy wax warmer. Instead of disposable liquid soap containers, pick up a really cute dispenser and some refills.

16. *Think temporary.*

If you do have temporary things, use them all up before you buy more. Which means that even if the scented candles are on a "buy two get ten free" sale, remind yourself that you have to burn all ten that you bought last year before you restock.

17. *Make do with multi-duty wrapping paper.*

Have a basic roll of wrapping paper that you use for every occasion. If you're more folksy, grab a roll of craft paper and use twine as ribbon. Or if you love to be a bit more dramatic, how about a roll of silver foil—that would work for a kid's birthday party or a wedding gift.

18. *Don't replace—reimagine.*

I've been using my bread maker religiously for the past year. Every week I make at least one loaf of bread and a batch of rolls for us to consume. But last week, my beloved bread maker decided it kneaded its last loaf.

I'd been reconsidering the whole bread maker for a couple of reasons. First, I use it only to knead the dough (I hated the tough loaves it baked). And second, it takes up a lot of room on my kitchen counter. I decided it was worth having on the counter since I used it at least twice a week, but given its size, it definitely was an investment in counter space. And since it weighed in at over seventeen pounds, I had a semi-rational fear of dropping it on my toes every time I moved it.

But when I recently put the ingredients in it and it failed to whirl to life, I decided it was time to try a new method—dough by KitchenAid. I pulled out the bread pan and dumped the ingredients into my Kitchen-Aid bowl. Following some instructions I found online, I was able to rescue the dough. The good news? The rolls turned out better mixed in the KitchenAid than in the bread maker. I just reclaimed a huge chunk of counter space and saved a hundred dollars at the same time.

What could you do without? When your alarm clock dies, do you really need a new one, or does the alarm on your cell phone suffice? When your TV dies, do you need to replace it, or do you watch everything on your computer anyway?

19. *"Buy one get one free" is not your friend.*

Yes, it may be in certain cases (some food items and things like laundry detergent). But if you are buying an extra just to get one free, make sure it is actually something you will use. "Buy one get one free" helps you only if it's something you'll use. But buy an ink cartridge and get this flashlight shaped like a race car for free is not a good clutter-reducing plan.

20. *Have a beneficiary.*

My daughter, Kimberly, is on a budget. As in a "can I come over and raid your fridge so I can use my money to put gas in my car to make it to work" kind of budget. So if I get a free gift with purchase, a free sample of foo-foo shampoo, or a little gift from a speaking engagement that is a duplicate of something I already have, I love to pass those things along to her. (And that child who wouldn't eat leftovers or wear her sister's hand-me-downs at sixteen is magically super grateful for that box of tea or sample facial mask as a broke twenty-two-year-old.)

I have a little area where I put all the things that Kim (or my stepdaughter, Amanda) might be interested in adopting. But they are also good at saying no to the things they won't use or love. That way I can be assured that I'm never burdening them with my clutter.

21. *Multipurpose is multi-fabulous.*

In *The Get Yourself Organized Project*, I made a list of everything I have on my kitchen counter. (I believe that the kitchen counter is the most valuable real estate of almost any house.) In that list I included a toaster and a toaster oven. (Just typing those names out, I should have known I was doubling up.) A reader asked, "Why do you have a toaster and a toaster oven both? Couldn't your toaster oven do everything your toaster does?" I had never really thought about it. We are now toasterless and we've never looked back.

22. *Get rid of stock-up mentality.*

I used to think that when something was on sale, I had to buy a hundred of those items. But the truth is that there will always be another big sale. And there will always be more toothpaste. So yes, let yourself have one or two extra tubes for one of those late-night emergencies, but don't fill your cabinets with stuff just because it's a good deal or you think you might need it.

23. *Go neutral with your decorating.*

If you have a turquoise couch and an orange carpet, you are stuck with that color scheme and will always feel tempted to buy (and hoard) things that match it. Plus, come Christmas when your color scheme may be red and green, you'll have to totally redecorate. Instead, save up for a tan couch, a gray rug, and a brown coffee table and then decorate with a few fun punches of color that can change with the seasons.

24. *Go neutral with your beauty.*

Pick up a few, essential items in neutral colors (white nail polish, a black headband) and then get rid of all the stuff that matches only one outfit. The same goes for shoes, although I'm never going to be the one to tell you that you don't need those red cowboy boots.

25. *Experiment.*

Is your mug shelf making you mad? Pack up half of those bad boys and see what you miss. If you just can't live without your limited edition *Doctor Who* TARDIS mug (with removable lid), awesome—go dig it out of the box. But if you find you don't miss any of those mugs, pack them up and send them to Goodwill where someone will cherish your oversized *Rugrats* drinking cup.

26. *Know yourself.*

When you know you look pale in pink, dumpy in A-line skirts, and hate anything peppermint, you will be less tempted by dirt-cheap sales on things you know you won't love. That pink A-line skirt on sale for eight dollars is no bargain if you know you'll never wear it. Give the peppermint tea that came in a holiday gift basket to a friend. To thine own self be uncluttered.

27. *Make your decor do double duty.*

I used to have a table runner for every holiday. Now? I have one that's red. It works for Christmas, New Years, Thanksgiving, and the Fourth of July. Sure, I have a box with a few frips and frills, but I'm no longer behaving as if I'm decorating the Bergdorf Goodman Holiday Windows (which they work on year-round). I keep it simple and pretty and have to be creative because I'm not buying to impress, I'm creating to enjoy.

28. *Rotate your inventory.*

Make sure your storage areas are for storing things you actually use, not just things you don't want to deal with. I have a few tubs in the garage that get switched out every six or seven months: Out-of-Season

Clothes, Out-of-Season Shoes, Out-of-Season Linens. About April or May I get down all those boxes and liberate my sandals, linen pants, and cotton sheets and pack up my wooly scarves, heavy jackets, and flannel sheets. It keeps my closets and drawers from being overrun, and it's like getting together with an old friend after six months apart. You never appreciate your cute silver flip-flops more than when your feet have been trapped in dark-brown leather boots for months on end.

29. *Co-own.*
    If your brothers, sisters, brothers- and sisters-in-law, or parents all live in the same town, you don't all need to own chafing dishes, a dog carrier, and a copy of *Citizen Cane.* I know some families who have gone in together on motor homes, vacation homes, dirt bikes, and ATVs.

30. *Make a clutter-free donation as a gift.*
    One Christmas, our family decided to give "stuff free" gifts. My kids chipped in and, through World Vision, bought me the sponsorship of a goat for a family in a developing country. To represent the gift, my daughters found instructions online to fold a towel into the shape of a goat (like the towel sculptures the cabin stewards make on cruise ships). Generous hearts and no stuff.

31. *Keep a donation bin in your car.*
    And make it a weekly task to drop things off at Goodwill.

32. *Give a cooking lesson as a nonclutter gift.*
    Give cooking lessons as a gift instead of something else that will clutter. Not only is a cooking class something you can do with a spouse or a friend, you'll finally discover which of all those kitchen tools you've been hoarding you actually need to keep.

33. *Focus on one hobby at a time.*
    Don't collect hobbies. For so many of us buying the tools is actually more fun that doing the hobby. Only one hobby at a time ensures you don't buy scads of yarn for knitting when in reality you are spending all your time working on your latest watercolors.

34. *Give a national park pass.*

Give a family member a gift that gets all of you out of the house (or suggest this to Grandma when she asks what to get your family for Christmas). Think nonclutter!

35. *Break your mall habit.*

We are shopaholics. Reports show that shopping malls have become the third most frequented location for Americans, after home and work.

If you're going there "just to window shop," statistics say that you may be fooling yourself:

- 75 percent of all Americans visit a mall at least once a month.

- Shopping malls have become community centers for social and recreational activities.

- On average, shoppers visit 3.4 times per month and stay 1 hour and 24 minutes.

- The average number of stores entered per visit is two.

- On average, a purchase is made in nearly half of all stores visited.

- 81 percent of all shoppers make at least one purchase each visit.

- 34.5 percent of all shoppers are browsers, and they spend an average of $128.36 per trip.

(www.jcdecauxna.com/mall/document/mall-phenomenon)

36. *Refuse the bag.*

In some US cities, single-use carryout bags are now illegal (city ordinance), so the people who live there are in the habit of carrying a few reusable bags in their car or purse. That or they end up with groceries all over the back of the car. According to some of my friends who live in these cities, it's nice to not have stacks of paper or plastic bags lying around their house.

37. *Buy used when you can.*

Used items rarely come with packaging that you have to dispose of.

38. *Don't get a storage unit.*

It's too easy to buy more stuff you don't need if there's extra room to store it. If you have a storage unit, realize it is one more thing draining your time, money, and energy. Find the ten items in there you really care about and get them out. Everything else—sell, give away, or donate.

39. *Refuse to renew.*

Don't renew subscriptions for those magazines that sit untouched each week as they come through your mail.

40. *Don't bring work home.*

This is impossible for some, but as much as you can keep your office in your office and out of your home, you are contributing to your peace of mind. I had one friend who left work early to beat traffic, and then he would work at home for ninety minutes. Or at least that was the plan. Turned out he would spend a few hours every night on work stuff, seriously ruining any free time he had. Finally, he resolved that the only thing he would bring home from the office was his laptop. No papers, no charger. His battery would last about two hours, so he had to have his work completed and saved long before the battery ran out. He did admit that he had an emergency charger, but he made it so inconvenient to get to that he would dig it out only if there was a real emergency.

41. *Make a spending plan.*

Require a two-person agreement—you and your spouse must agree on the purchase before you spend X amount of dollars on something. This could stop a lot of mall trips.

42. *Ask yourself, "In three years will I be glad that I bought this today?"*

43. *Ask yourself, "If I buy a new book, am I willing to get rid of two that I've read? If not, is this book worth buying?"*

44. *Ask yourself, "Where will this be placed in the house when I get it home?"*

If you can't think of a place (or of what you'll get rid of to make room for it), then think twice before it becomes clutter.

45. *Ask yourself, "If my spouse were with me, would I still spend the money on this?"*

This keeps me from about 20 percent of all my potential purchases.

46. *No more tubs.*

Go for a year without buying any storage tubs, organizers, see-through shoe boxes, or any other containers for your items. Instead, get rid of as much stuff as possible and use the storage tubs, organizers, see-through shoe boxes, or any other containers you already have to store your stuff.

47. *Leave it in the car.*

I don't bring trash into the house. If it's in the car, I leave it in the car until I am either heading to my garbage can or can clean it out while at a gas station.

48. *Recycle your mail ASAP.*

My paper recycling bin is directly next to my mailbox in my garage. Probably close to 80 percent of my mail never even goes into the house. A word of caution here: You'll want to be sure to shred any junk mail, such as credit card applications, that contain any personal information.

49. *Make tea instead of buying bottles of it.*

50. *Imagine your home clean and clutter free.*

That feeling is worth more than anything you are holding in your hand to purchase.

A Final Word

Dear Friends,

As I finish up this book, I do it in the midst of stuff. My dad is now under hospice care, and we're in the process of saying goodbye. What we have left to deal with is the stuff of my dad's life.

Amid the piles of magazines, CDs, computer parts, and stamps (oh, so much stuff) are the treasures of his life. The painting his mom did of him at Golden Gate Park when he was a young, single man. The letters he wrote to me, and received from me, when I lived in Japan. The drawing a friend did of him with his face on a postage stamp. The picture of him with his first grandchild, my son Justen.

As I go through these things, I want you to be reminded of my heart behind this book: it's not simply to get rid of stuff, but to uncover and appreciate the treasures you already have.

My prayer is that yes, you reduce the clutter, but only so you can make room for the best things in your life: the people, the memories, the treasures that you love.

My hope is that you uncover things you thought were lost, and that when you find those things, you get to remember the stories of those things and the people you treasure so much.

Kathi

Appendix 1

The Three-Box, Two-Bag System

This is a system you will be using in almost every room in your house, so I want you to gather up everything that you'll need right now:

- Set up three cardboard boxes, a garbage bag, and a recycle bag, your iPod, and a timer (you can use the one on your cell phone or your oven).

- Mark one cardboard box "Other Rooms," one "Put Back," and one "Give Away."

- Give yourself fifteen minutes on your timer and pick a spot to clean out (an area no larger than what you can sort through in fifteen minutes).

- Go through the area and use the three boxes to sort the contents.

Other Rooms Box

Anything that doesn't belong in the area you're cleaning goes into the "Other Rooms" box. This includes toys in the kitchen, dog brushes in the living room, report cards in the bathroom, or dishes in the bedroom.

Put Back Box

This is the box where you put things that belong in the area you're cleaning, but they need to be put back in the right place. If you're straightening up your bedroom, examples of items that you would place in this box are clean clothes on the floor, shoes under your bed, or scarves hanging over a bedroom chair. These all go in the "Put Back" box so once you have your bedroom in order, you just put those items back where they belong.

Give Away Box

Clothes your kids have outgrown? Check. Videos your family will never watch again? Check. There is huge freedom in giving stuff away. Here is a great set of criteria for keeping or giving away an item:

- Is it something you or a family member is currently using or wearing?
- Is it something that makes you or a family member happy when they see it?
- Is it something you or a family member will definitely use in the next six months?

If you can answer yes to one or more of those questions, find a home for the item. If not, away it goes.

And a friendly reminder: don't donate garbage. It costs charities time and money to get rid of stuff that you don't want. Don't be that person. Donate only those things that are in decent condition and are worthy of reselling.

Garbage Bag

Anything that you don't want and that isn't worthy of being donated or can't be recycled goes in here.

Recycle Bag

Recycling regulations vary from city to city, so check with your local municipality or disposal service if you have any question about what should be recycled and what shouldn't.

Once you've cleaned out your chosen area, take the "Other Rooms" box and go around the house putting away all the stuff in that box. Take the "Give Away" box to where you gather stuff to donate or directly to your car to be donated the next time you run errands. Now, since your area is clean and organized, put anything in the "Put Back" box into the spot it's supposed to go.

If this feels totally overwhelming to you, consider having a supportive friend or someone you hire go through these steps for you. There's a lot of freedom in a fresh start.

Appendix 2

A Simple System for Dealing with Paperwork

Paperwork. Is there any word that more frequently causes us to groan internally than the word *paperwork*? Ugh.

When computers made their appearance, we were all teased with the idea of the "paperless society." What it really meant was that anyone with a computer and a printer could cheaply churn out even more paperwork that I now have to deal with.

But I want to give you hope. You don't have to be overrun, overwhelmed, or feel as though you are in over your head anymore. I have a simple system that has turned me from someone who paid my bills late, forgot about dentist appointments, and lost receipts, to the woman who can find most things most of the time. (Hey, I didn't say I had a magic wand.)

Step 1: Your Plan of Attack

I strongly suggest you gather all your loose paper into one place—every mail pile in your living room, all those magazines you want to save but aren't sure why, the random sticky notes, coupons, envelopes.

Search every nook and cranny around your house, and everything that was once a tree (except for your furniture) goes in the box.

If you're dealing with more than one box of papers, perhaps you should limit yourself to fifteen minutes of sorting at a time so as not to become overwhelmed. (I know that large stacks of paper make me want to roll up in a ball in a corner and weep uncontrollably.)

Step 2: Sort It Out

If you're not familiar with my three-box, two-bag organizing system, this would be a good time to get acquainted with it (see appendix 1). For dealing with paperwork, you'll want to use those three boxes, but I hope you'll need only one bag because you are able to recycle paper in your community. You'll also want an additional box—a "Life Organization File (LOF)" box. More on that soon.

Other Rooms Box

Sometimes you need to move papers to other places—perhaps an order form needs to be put in your son's backpack, or you have something that needs to be mailed right away. Maybe you need your husband to look over an invitation, or directions to tomorrow's board meeting need to go into your purse. Great, put those in this box and make some time to get all the paperwork where it needs to be.

Put Back Box

This box is for anything that you need to file. Every household should have a simple filing system for receipts, warranties, tax returns, and all those other papers that aren't currently "in motion" but may need to be referred to at a later date.

Try to keep your files as lean and mean as possible. You don't need to keep your check stubs from college or warranties from a fridge you no longer own. Since so much of our lives are stored on our computers, we can get rid of a lot of the paperwork we no longer need. You can find most instruction manuals online, scan articles to keep on your computer, and put reminders directly on your digital calendar.

If you have extensive files, I suggest a great book to you. *Getting*

Things Done by David Allen has a no-nonsense plan for keeping your files usable.

Examine whether you need more than one drawer of file storage. Perhaps if you work at home or if you have a spouse who loves doing the bills and keeps everything, fine. If it's working for you, great. If it's not, try getting rid of most of your paper.

Create for yourself a Life Organization File box. This box is for any papers that are currently in play. In this box, place the stuff like tickets to the theater and insurance paperwork that needs to be mailed. In just a bit, I'm going to tell you what to do with all that paper.

Give Away Box

Do you have magazines that your library or some other organization would love? Ask first, and then drop them off.

Recycling Bag (and Garbage Bag if needed)

You shouldn't have much for the garbage, but I suggest a shredder for any sensitive information you want to get rid of.

Step 3: Clean It Up

Whatever area you just gathered up your paperwork from, can I make a suggestion? Give it a good cleaning, and then put something beautiful there. If you just uncovered your kitchen counter from a pile of papers, don't leave that space blank—put a beautiful bowl, a vase, a basket of fruit, something there so that you will be reminded to never pile up those papers again.

Step 4: Label It and Put It Away

Papers you need to retrieve later go in the file drawer. Papers you still need to work on go into your Life Organization File (LOF).

The Life Organization File

If you're anything like me, you have a million "notes to self," and every once in a while a little piece of paper can get lost in your shuffle. I have found a very simple system that can help even the most hopelessly unorganized person amaze her friends and family with clever holiday ideas and on-time birthday greetings (as well as getting the bills paid on time). Here are the items you'll need, most of which you probably have on hand:

- one file box
- twelve hanging files with tabs
- thirty-one file folders
- one permanent marker
- sticky notes
- your home calendar
- your home address book
- a book of stamps

Putting Your Life Organization File Together

On each of the tabs of the twelve hanging files write one of the months of the year (January–December) and on each of the file folders, the days of the month (1–31).

Put all the month files in the back of your file box, and the 1–31 folders in the front.

Using Your Life Organization File

Once your file is put together, the hardest part is over. Now all you have to do is use it.

For Everyday Life

1. Set aside some time at the beginning of your week to file the paperwork that needs it. I do paperwork on Mondays, so any bills, information the kids bring home from school, sales flyers, coupons, etc. that show up the week before go into the coming Monday's file folder. Say that Monday is the 14th. I have a sticky note that I put on folder 14 to

remind me that's where I'll put all the papers I will be filing on that day.

2. Monday the 14th I go through all those papers, work on them or file them, and then move the sticky note to folder 21—the next Monday when I will be doing paperwork. Here are some examples of things I do with those little slips of paper:

   • Make a list of errands

   • See what sales are coming up

   • Note bills that need to be paid (or filed for later)

   • Jot down things I need to put on the calendar

I check to see if I can (or must) take care of any of these items immediately. When I open my mail, I always do it with my recycle basket, calendar, and Life Organization File (LOF) right next to me. Dates get entered on the calendar, papers are recycled, and forms, bills, and important paperwork are dropped into the LOF.

So, say you have a pile of papers just sitting on your desk. Here is how I would go through that pile with my LOF:

• *Bills*—Put these in the coming Monday's file.

• *Invitation to a party two months away on October 10*—Put that in the October file. When you get to October, you will put everything in that file into the numbered file folders.

• *Sales flyers*—Put those in next Monday's file so you can create your shopping list based on what's on sale.

Some Additional Tips

• You know how you come across a great recipe for Christmas cookies on January 15? Clip out that recipe and drop it in your December file. It will be waiting for you next holiday season.

- Find the perfect Maxine card for your sister, but her birthday is still months away? Buy it now (saving you an emergency trip to the store) and place it in her birthday month's file.

- See a great article on the Internet on flowerpot painting and want to try it out when you visit your mom in May? Just drop it in the May file, and you'll remember to take it with you.

- Once a year I go on a greeting-card buying spree. I buy cards that are just right for the people in my life, and some general ones to have on hand. Dayspring.com is a great resource for general cards. When I get the cards home, I address them and stamp the envelopes, but do not sign them until I'm ready to mail them. I want my greetings to be fresh and interesting.

- This filing system also makes a great gift for an older family member who likes to send cards. Show them your file first to see if it's something they would use. Some of my relatives in their nineties have better memories than I do and have no need for a file system!

- When I look through a catalog and see a gift idea, I rip it out and put it in the appropriate file. Even if I don't end up purchasing that exact item, it's nice to have ideas.

- The files are a great place to store directions to events such as weddings and parties. You can even keep tickets to future events in the appropriate month's file (instead of having them hang out on the fridge for four months).

I also have a selection of thank-you notes, thinking-of-you cards, and a few sympathy cards on hand for last-minute needs.

Step 5: Keep It Up

Set aside one day a week to do all your paperwork. If it's Wednesday, and this week Wednesday falls on the 14th, then all that week leading

up to Wednesday, just drop any paperwork into the folder marked "14."
I flag that folder with a giant sticky note so it's easy to drop papers into
for review. Once I'm done with that Wednesday, I move the sticky note
to the next Wednesday.

Using Your Space, Time, Energy, and Money Well

Space

So much for our paperless society, right? However, I do scan many
items and file them on my computer. One piece of paper doesn't take
up a lot of room, but when you multiply that by all the notes, reminders, mementos, and articles, we're talking binders' worth of paper.

Time

When it comes to paperwork, my biggest time-saver is something
I call "Putting It Back into Play." When I get a piece of paper that
requires an action (putting it on my calendar, paying it, returning it
to a teacher, getting it back to church), my goal is to get that piece of
paper "back into play" as quickly as possible by noting it on my calendar and then recycling the notice, writing the check, and sending the
bill back in the same day's mail, or signing that permission slip and putting it in my daughter's backpack. The LOF is for anything that I can't
deal with on the spot, so instead of letting the papers pile up on the
kitchen counter, I place them in the file to deal with on a certain day.
But if I can "Put It Back into Play" right away, then I've saved myself
some additional steps. Big win!

I don't want that piece of paper fermenting in my house. Anytime
a piece of paper sits around, it gets heavier. There are now fines to pay,
excuses to make, and apologies to write. I want to get that ball into
someone else's court, not to give them more work, but so they're no
longer waiting on me to do their work.

Energy

Moving piles of paper takes energy. Don't let a piece of paper sit on
your desk or counter; it invites friends. Get that paper back into play.

Money

Not being organized paper-wise comes with a financial cost. Late bills, last-minute trips to drop permission slips at school, lost checks, lost rebates, coupons that expire—they all total up to hundreds (if not thousands) of dollars lost each year.

Appendix 3

Cheri's Packing List

*I*n chapter 10, "Just in Case," I talked about my friend Cheri's trip to Europe and how she managed to get by with one small suitcase. For those of you who are curious about how she got by with so little, here is her brief overview and a list of the items she packed for her trip.

Two items still have tags and are being returned. Three items got worn only once and I wish I'd left them home. I couldn't believe how long I was able to stretch "travel size" items like mousse and hair spray.

I had no access to a washing machine, though I did a bit of hand laundry and hung items out on balconies each night. I turned in one bag of laundry on the cruise, which was great except it came back without my favorite nightgown.

Here's the complete list, which doesn't include what was in my computer bag:

- Running shoes (wore during air travel only)
- Black flats (wore during five university visits)
- Orthaheel flip-flops (wore *all the time*)
- Worlds Softest Socks (two pair that I wore during air travel only)

- Athletic socks (two pair that I never wore)
- Sleeveless tops—black, black-and-white, pink, blue (wore each two or three times; ended up using black for sleeping
- Sleeveless top—red (didn't look good with sunburn, will return)
- Bathing suit (used only once but was well worth it!)
- Cargo crops—khaki (wore four or five times, mostly morning and evening when it was cooler or once we'd gotten to a hotel with air-conditioning)
- Cargo crops—black (didn't need and will return; already had black slacks and yoga pants)
- Jeans (wore for air travel only)
- Nice black slacks (wore three times—two university visits and one dinner on cruise)
- Yoga pants (wore for hanging out and for sleep if the room was cold)
- Skorts—black and putty (wore daily when touring outdoor locations—it was *hot!*)
- Polo shirts—pink and navy (wore two or three times)
- Black cap-sleeve top, sorta dressy (wore three or four times, mostly in the evening)
- Neutral cap-sleeve top (wore five or six times; lightweight, fit well, washed and dried with ease)
- Black sweater (had two and kept one with me at all times; wore when visiting a university after a morning of touring and needed to dress up my informal outfit)
- Black long-sleeved casual top (slept in it when the room was cold; wore on the way home)
- Purple three-quarter-sleeve dressy top (wore on the way there; wore a few times in evenings)

- Dressy purple-and-white, short-sleeved top (wore to one university)
- Purple dressy cardigan (wore to one university)
- Colorful skirt (hoped purple cardigan would match but it did *not*; wore to one university)
- Travel alarm clock (we had three alarms each morning)
- Apple travel adapter kit
- Sewing kit
- Toiletries—liquid-based in large Ziploc
- Toiletries—nonliquid in small Ziploc

Dear Reader,

Thanks for being a part of *Clutter Free*. One of the greatest privileges I have is to hear back from the people who have used my books. I would love to stay in touch.

Website: www.KathiLipp.com
Facebook: facebook.com/authorkathilipp
Twitter: twitter.com/kathilipp
Mail: Kathi Lipp
171 Branham Lane
Suite 10-122
San Jose, CA 95136

In His Grace,

Kathi Lipp

Other Books by Kathi Lipp

The Get Yourself Organized Project
21 Steps to Less Mess and Stress

Finally, an organizational book for women who have given up trying to be Martha Stewart but still desire some semblance of order in their lives.

Most organizational books are written by and for people who are naturally structured and orderly. For the woman who is more ADD than type A, the advice sounds terrific but seldom works. These women are looking for help that takes into account their free-spirited outlook while providing tips and tricks they can easily follow to live a more organized life.

Kathi Lipp, author of *The Husband Project* and other "project" books, is just the author to address this need. In her inimitable style, she offers

- easy and effective ways you can restore peace to your everyday life
- simple and manageable long-term solutions for organizing any room in your home (and keeping it that way)
- a realistic way to de-stress a busy schedule
- strategies for efficient shopping, meal preparation, cleaning, and more

Full of helpful tips and abundant good humor, *The Get Yourself Organized Project* will enable you to spend your time living and enjoying life rather than organizing your sock drawer.

The Husband Project
21 Days of Loving Your Man— on Purpose and with a Plan

Keeping your marriage healthy is all about the details—the daily actions and interactions in which you lift each other up and offer support, encouragement, and love. In *The Husband Project* you will discover fun and creative ways to bring back that lovin' feeling and remind your husband—and yourself—why you married in the first place.

Using the sense of humor that draws thousands of women a year to hear her speak, Kathi Lipp shows you through simple daily action plans how you can bring the fun back into your relationship even amidst your busy schedules.

The Husband Project is an indispensable resource that will help you to

- discover the unique plan God has for your marriage and your role as a wife
- create a plan to love your husband "on purpose"
- support and encourage other wives who want to make their marriage a priority
- experience release from the guilt of "not being enough"

If you desire to bring more joy into your marriage but just need a little help setting a plan into action, *The Husband Project* is for you.

The "What's for Dinner?" Solution
Quick, Easy, and Affordable Meals Your Family Will Love

For many women, dread turns to panic around 4:00 in the afternoon. That's when they have to answer that age-old question, "What's for dinner?" Many resort to another supermarket rotisserie chicken or—worse yet—ordering dinner through a drive-thru intercom.

The "What's for Dinner?" Solution provides a full-kitchen approach for getting dinner on the table every night. After putting Kathi's 21-day plan into action, you will

- save time—with bulk shopping and cooking
- save money—no more last-minute phone calls to the delivery pizza place
- save your sanity—forget the last-minute scramble every night and know what you're having for dinner

The book includes real recipes from real women, a quick guide to planning meals for a month, the best shopping strategies for saving time and money, and tips on the best ways to use a slow cooker, freezer, and pantry.

With Kathi's book in hand, there's no more need to hit the panic button.

Happy Habits for Every Couple
21 Days to a Better Relationship

When was the last time you flirted with your husband? Was it before you had kids?

Do you spend more time on the couch with your wife watching movies or with a bag of chips watching The Game?

Does your idea of a hot date include a drive-thru and springing for the extra-large fries?

What would your marriage look like if for 21 days you turned your attention to happy habits that will better your relationship? Plenty of books describe how to improve a marriage, how to save a marriage, even how to ramp up intimacy in a marriage. In *Happy Habits for Every Couple*, Kathi Lipp and husband Roger show you practical, fun-filled ways to put love and laughter back into your marriage.

Here are just a few of the results you'll see when you put *Happy Habits for Every Couple* into practice:

- new levels of warmth and tenderness in your relationship
- a deeper sense of security with your spouse
- a marriage filled with fun and flirting

If you haven't given up the dream of being head-over-heels with your spouse again, following this 21-day plan will give you just the boost you need to bring you closer together.

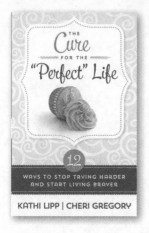

The Cure for the "Perfect" Life

12 Ways to Stop Trying Harder and Start Living Braver

Are you crumbling under the burden of perfection? You know the expectations are unreasonable—even unreachable. And when everyone else seems more together than you, where do you turn for help?

Meet Kathi, a disguised perfectionist always looking to put everyone else's needs above her own, and Cheri, a formerly confused and exhausted poster girl for playing it safe. They've struggled just like you—and found the cure. With unabashed empathy and humor, they invite you to take part in their rebellion against perfection.

Step-by-step they'll teach you how to challenge and change unhealthy beliefs. As they free you from always seeking more or needing approval of others, you'll discover a new, braver way of living. At last, you'll exchange outdated views of who you *should be* for a clearer vision of *who you are* in Christ.

The truth is you don't have to be perfect. You just have to be brave enough to read this book.

To learn more about Harvest House books and
to read sample chapters, visit our website:

www.harvesthousepublishers.com

HARVEST HOUSE PUBLISHERS
EUGENE, OREGON